Public Administration and Information Technology

Volume 2

Series Editor

Christopher G. Reddick

For further volumes:
http://www.springer.com/series/10796

Jeffrey Roy

From Machinery to Mobility

Government and Democracy
in a Participative Age

 Springer

HUMBER LIBRARIES LAKESHORE CAMPUS
3199 Lakeshore Blvd West
TORONTO, ON.   M8V 1K8

Jeffrey Roy
Dalhousie University
Halifax, Nova Scotia
Canada

ISBN 978-1-4614-7220-9   ISBN 978-1-4614-7221-6 (eBook)
DOI 10.1007/978-1-4614-7221-6
Springer New York Heidelberg Dordrecht London

Library of Congress Control Number: 2013936397

© Springer Science+Business Media New York 2013
This work is subject to copyright. All rights are reserved by the Publisher, whether the whole or part of the material is concerned, specifically the rights of translation, reprinting, reuse of illustrations, recitation, broadcasting, reproduction on microfilms or in any other physical way, and transmission or information storage and retrieval, electronic adaptation, computer software, or by similar or dissimilar methodology now known or hereafter developed. Exempted from this legal reservation are brief excerpts in connection with reviews or scholarly analysis or material supplied specifically for the purpose of being entered and executed on a computer system, for exclusive use by the purchaser of the work. Duplication of this publication or parts thereof is permitted only under the provisions of the Copyright Law of the Publisher's location, in its current version, and permission for use must always be obtained from Springer. Permissions for use may be obtained through RightsLink at the Copyright Clearance Center. Violations are liable to prosecution under the respective Copyright Law.
The use of general descriptive names, registered names, trademarks, service marks, etc. in this publication does not imply, even in the absence of a specific statement, that such names are exempt from the relevant protective laws and regulations and therefore free for general use.
While the advice and information in this book are believed to be true and accurate at the date of publication, neither the authors nor the editors nor the publisher can accept any legal responsibility for any errors or omissions that may be made. The publisher makes no warranty, express or implied, with respect to the material contained herein.

Printed on acid-free paper

Springer is part of Springer Science+Business Media (www.springer.com)

Preface

Government today is akin to an experienced sailing crew facing uncharted and volatile waters: the accumulated skills and wisdom are enough to stay afloat, but the strain and leaks are spreading. As Norah Jones sings, "With a captain who's too proud to say, that he dropped the oar....we're gonna be sinkin' soon."

Perhaps not sinking, but in many countries the ship that is government requires refurbishment: suspicion and cynicism are on the rise both within and on the outside as more and more question the resilience and performance of its present incarnation. In short, the sturdy machinery of government stemming from pre-digital and highly autocratic and often aristocratic eras—with scarcity of education and information the norm—is poorly suited to contemporary realities and the still-nascent but ever more visible and influential era of mobility.

As this book neared completion over the summer of 2012, three sets of diverging forces are illustrative of what drives this particular undertaking—and the nature of the challenges presenting themselves.

First, within Dalhousie University's blended learning MPA (M) Program, an online dialogue with current public servants explored the tension between traditional Westminster government principles and practices and the emergence of so-called Government 2.0 (as discussed below, closely related to Web 2.0 and the advent of mobility). Working collaboratively and virtually, students prepared prototypes of new governance models crafted upon a Gov 2.0 mindset, many utilizing social media and wikis for the first time. In highly focused policy and service realms, the projects demonstrated the collective potential of a more outward and agile public sector no longer seeking control but instead opportunities to listen, learn, and act in concert with others.

Along with this considerable promise nonetheless came the cold shower of the final exam. Asked to examine the systemic barriers to the embracement of what some researchers have termed "ubiquitous engagement" (Lee and Kwak 2011), students dissected the command and control political architecture democratically and its close bureaucratic cousin administratively. The broad lesson learned is as follows: the space in between tradition and structures of the past—and the potentials of tomorrow—remains vast. This book seeks to dissect and explain this space and its repercussions for the public sector in terms of both management and democracy.

Secondly—and from outside of government—stories abound with regard to how mobile technologies and the proliferation of smartphones are fundamentally altering the way we live and behave. Some are wildly enthusiastic in embracing such change; others have growing doubts as to what may be lost. For example, in late July of 2012 New York Times technology writer, David Pogue, lost his iPhone and in an effort to locate it proceeded to leverage the collective engagement of nearly 1.4 million Twitter followers—as well as the digital tracking functionality of the device itself (the Find My iPhone app that uses GPS signalling). Acting on numerous tips and the social media frenzy that ensued, a police officer retrieved it from a New Jersey backyard (Pogue 2012).

When asked about the privacy implications of such digital footprints, Pogue replied with indifference, arguing that sacrificing privacy is a modest, reasonable price for the gains of digital life. He pointed to credit card transactions, telephone surveillance, and public and industry data mining as the new norms of being on the grid—with the considerable benefits of convenience and innovation (and we can add, collective action) resulting. In short, Pogue pointed out that in today's digital world, there really is no disconnecting from such ubiquity, so why not embrace it?

Why not indeed? Yet just a few days later, a very different perspective from a Washington Post writer featuring a tech savvy individual's decision to retreat from the digital fast lane of Silicon Valley into a small town setting—and a primarily offline life (Timberg 2012). Seeking calmer, quieter surroundings for creativity and more traditional and meaningful forms of community engagement, a former Facebook user and employee, Katherine Losse, touched a nerve for many in conveying a sense of disquiet and anxiety that many experience in today's world, but few are able or willing to articulate, even as this movement is growing (Losse 2012).

Whether innovation is driven by solitude or incessant socialization as well as impacts from an online world blending personal and professional spheres to an unprecedented degree is central to an evolving workplace and demographic cleavages shaping it. Such matters, in short, are central to mobility and the present quest for Government 2.0.

Thirdly, while the trials and tribulations of Facebook and Research in Motion captured many business headlines in 2012, the main battle in the technology world was playing out in court rooms and retail stores around the world—namely, the intensifying rivalry between Apple and Android as the operating system of choice for smartphones and tablets. The most visible legal dispute stemming from this battle has featured patent infringement disputes between Apple and Samsung (the latter the most prominent Android user in its smartphone and tablet devices). Apple would win the August 2012 ruling; Samsung immediately appealed and days later also won a separate ruling in Japan.

For the public sector, this epic clash of technology titans encapsulates upheaval in traditional procurement and IT management models due to the advent of cloud computing, social media, and smart devices. Along with shifting notions of ownership in terms of infrastructure, governments have been quick to embrace "open data" and the development of "apps" as a means of collective, 2.0-stylized forms of engagement. The somewhat analogous clashes between proprietary and open source technologically, and information control and genuine openness politically and administratively, are central to widening schisms between machinery and mobility visions of the public sector uncomfortably coexisting at present.

In dissecting these and other tensions, a strong case emerges for a holistic reconfiguration of democratic and administrative governance. The aim of this book project is less fundamental resolution of such complex terrain and more providing (1) some informed guidance as to the sorts of choices and challenges that must be met, (2) a critical assessment of government efforts thus far, and (3) some insights and lessons as to how creative and collective adaptation can best be nurtured and leveraged as digital life expands. This book similarly serves as a platform for postsecondary students of government in moving beyond traditional notions of *machinery of government* and devising—collectively and creatively—new models of more open and participative governance premised upon *mobility*. The contrasts and cleavage between machinery and mobility are central to contemporary public sector life. This book, then, seeks a basis for charting swirling and unknown waters.

Many are deserving of thanks and gratitude for their input and support as this book took shape. Some core themes of this book were initially explored in the preparation of a background report for the OECD, as part of their efforts to explore and better understand mobility and agility in the public sector: thank you to Barbara-Chiara Ubaldi for this opportunity. A shared undertaking with Greg Lane of CISCO Systems also proved similarly enlightening, as have insights shared by Ashley Casovan of the City of Edmonton, Dave Conabree of the Government of Canada, and Nancy MacLellan of the Province of Nova Scotia. I must also gratefully acknowledge the support of Dalhousie's School of Public Administration and the efforts in particular of Kevin Quigley to preserve a culture of research despite significant crosswinds in doing so. I benefitted from the dedicated research assistance of Obbia Barni, the thoughtful input of the blind reviewers, as well as the friendly professionals of Springer Publications (and series editor, Chris Reddick). Finally, a sincere note of thanks to Amanda Coe, Dan Belanger, and Valerie Troude for their friendship and generosity throughout (and to the t-bear who once again managed to sleep through it all).

Halifax, NS, Canada   Jeffrey Roy

Contents

Chapter 1
Introduction

Mobility? Think Mindset Not Handset.

Sue Norris[1]

The Mobility Mindset

Governments around the world are seeking to leverage digital technologies in order to improve operational and democratic governance: both promise and peril await. The still nascent era of mobility—further defined below though characterized by the expansion of cloud computing platforms, social media venues, and smaller and more portable and powerful "smart" devices—challenges many of the traditional structures and values that have come to shape politics, public sector operations, and the changing interface between the two.

Despite frequent invocations of "Government 2.0" in line with the rise of Web 2.0 as a more participative and user-centric version of Internet life, an alternative and equally relevant depiction of the public sector's digital evolution suggests that we are now witnessing the third and by far the most significant wave of reform.

The first wave, rooted in the rise of mainframe computers, was all about *processing*: what are now commonly referred to as legacy systems in order to underpin large-scale data operations in the back office. For governments, this meant electronically processing large-scale payment systems such as tax refunds, pension payments, unemployment and social assistance, etc. Much of the frontend of such public programs remained paper driven (with a significant amount of paper remaining today), underpinned by in-person, telephony, and traditional mail channels.

---

[1] Sue Norris is a technology industry journalist in the UK. Though no year is specified, this quote is featured in a series of quotes provided online: http://img2.insight.com/graphics/uk/media/pdf/inquotes-mobility.pdf

J. Roy, *From Machinery to Mobility: Government and Democracy in a Participative Age*,
Public Administration and Information Technology 2, DOI 10.1007/978-1-4614-7221-6_1,
© Springer Science+Business Media New York 2013

Printing and processing also carried symbolic value: many politicians were nervous about transiting to direct-deposit schemes, fearing diminished credit in the eyes of the public relative to receiving a government-sanctioned cheque in the main. For public servants, the back-end large-scale processing era of computing aligned well with the bureaucratic paradigm of traditional public administration. IT enabled larger and routinized forms of information management according to rules and silos—and while desktop computers began to appear to facilitate such specialization, their usage was highly structured and routinized.

The second wave, built upon the emergence of the Internet through the 1990s and much of the previous decade, centered on *infrastructure*: new service delivery channels revolutionizing the online face or the frontend of government. The public would thus be fashioned as "customers" of the state, and with the rise of e-commerce across traditional retailers, financial service companies, and new online platforms such as Amazon, invariable comparisons to private sector operations quickly ensued. Driven by online channels, lauded for both efficiency and convenience, more integrated and bundled service offerings sought to surmount the silo logic of governmental organizational charts in favor of portals organized around life events, client streams, and other such prisms where cost efficiencies and service synergies may exist (Flumian, Coe and Kernaghan 2007; Roy 2006; Borins et al. 2007; Dutil et al. 2010).

While processing and infrastructure remain the central elements of an evermore digitized public sector, it is the advent of an additional, third wave of technological reform that encompasses not only governmental operations but a wider spectrum of societal behavior—namely, a *culture and mindset of mobility*. This movement features four interrelated dimensions that reflect important shifts in technology, demography, and governance:

1. The explosive growth of broadband capacity (network speeds have increased an estimated 18 million times over the last 15 years alone)
2. The proliferation of personal, handheld devices of all kinds (by 2015 there will be nearly as many mobile smart devices as living people on Earth)
3. The rapid expansion of both front- and back-end virtualization (most notably social media and cloud computing, respectively)
4. The emergence of a more digitally ubiquitous society and workplace where traditional boundaries between personal and professional spaces are increasingly blurred (Lane and Roy 2011)

Personal computing power continually grows in ways unimaginable just a few short decades ago. Indeed, such innovation means that children today find rotary phones only in museums and even recent products such as so-called netbooks (mini-laptops with basic processing power meant to facilitate online access to an extended array of tools and programs) are all but displaced by today's ultrathin laptops, on the one hand, and tablet devices on the other hand. The advent of high-speed broadband and wireless connectivity enables roaming devices to decouple access and location while also providing new opportunities for location-specific information and services to recast virtual and physical boundaries and interactions (Buckler and Majer 2008; Young 2012). Furthermore, the Internet facilitates a widening canvas of both transnational and virtual policy networks and communities (McNutt and Pal 2011).

Also significant in this shifting digital and sensual universe is the proliferation of online video transmission as a rival to traditional routes of audio and text. The explosion of Skype-based telephony and YouTube video sharing is emblematic here: by late 2011, an estimated 24 hours of video was being uploaded to YouTube each minute. In a café or airport today, it is no longer unusual to witness individuals (typically young) visually engaged in both conversation and imagery via a smart device. University instructors are similarly challenged to adapt teaching methods from traditional learning and delivery models as information abundance and multi-tasking reshape behavioral norms.

Moreover, in corporate and government realms, evermore affordable and increasingly more effective platforms and tools for videoconferencing are beginning to challenge more traditional conference call formats and call into question the necessity of business travel for in-person meetings. As Rubin argues in his articulation of a much smaller world where energy and virtual communication costs move dramatically and inversely, the world's thirst for a finite supply of oil (along with parallel shifts in attitudes toward lessening carbon usage) suggests that a tipping point with respect to travel costs and communications channels may not be far off (Rubin 2010).

"To the Cloud"[2]

As broadband and virtualization expand, so too does the potential to leverage online platforms not merely as channels for communication and exchange but also a means to organizing most any aspect of digital infrastructure—for both individuals and organizations. Such is the basis of cloud computing. While arrangements and models vary, the essence of cloud computing is the shifting of more and more aspects of computing capacity—including processing, storage, and software—from single-site facilities such as the desktop computer to the Internet (Wyld 2007).

For many users, the first and most relevant example of cloud computing is e-mail—and signing up for a service such as Microsoft's Hotmail or Google's Gmail (the latter upending the former over the past decade via enhanced functionality and near-limitless storage capacity). Thus, aside from exchanging messages, images, and files, such an online e-mail platform negates the need for backing up hard drives on an actual desktop or accompany external device. For an organization serving a clientele high in digital literacy and demands, most obviously a postsecondary institution, the advent of cloud-based e-mail solutions presents an enticing alternative to creating and maintaining an in-house e-mail platform of its own (itself

---

[2] This phrase was the centerpiece of a 2011 Microsoft marketing campaign, notable since in previous years the proprietary software giant personified machine and organizational-based processing power of the sort challenged by the advent of the cloud. The commercials personify a mainstream acceptance of cloud computing for personal and corporate usage.

often a mix of off-the-shelf tools and customized elements maintained and serviced by in-house staff and/or hired specialists working specifically on such a system).

Indeed, Google would begin offering Gmail variants to public sector clients such as universities at no charge for the software, meaning the basic platform, interface, and functionality including infinite online storage require no upfront costs and no maintenance charges (since the Google cloud platform is maintained by the company for its full range of users). In Canada, the University of Alberta would be the first to embrace a cloud e-mail platform—with several others actively exploring similar arrangements with Google or other like-minded cloud providers.

For universities and for any organization, most especially those within the public sector sphere, offsetting concerns typically focus first and foremost on privacy and security. While each university is obviously far too small to demand its own separate cloud (often deemed a "private" cloud in terms of specifying, to some degree, where and how the data is stored and processed), the calculus of risk is whether data and identity protection are best provided via an expert outfit such as Google or developed and maintained on a micro-basis within the confines of a single entity (albeit with limited assistance via the engagement of consultants).

There are also related questions about the trustworthiness of the cloud provider in holding vast amounts of personal data and how such information is not only protected from intruders but also utilized internally within the confines of what typically is a corporate provider. Consequently, whereas social media sites such as Facebook are facilitated by cloud-based storage and processing platforms, some sectors, notably government, may opt instead for a so-called private cloud—a shared and virtual infrastructure albeit one whose boundaries and usage are more limited often to augment security.

A decade ago, housing e-mail externally via cloud-based platform would have been dismissed by most any university and indeed by most large organizations in any sector. Today, notwithstanding much debate surrounding security and privacy (key themes of Chaps. 4–6), cloud computing systems now underpin much of online life, and most every government in the world is actively exploring, if not pursuing, a growing number of IT infrastructure segments via this route.

As the cloud has become a mainstream concept and platform closely intertwined with the spreading of digital smart devices and mobile Internet access, acceptance is growing albeit not without concerns and differentiated viewpoints both personally and corporately. For some, the notion of virtually storing personal and proprietary information elsewhere remains a risky and uncomfortable leap: where is the data, how is it being stored and secured, and who has access to it are questions that loom large for governments with respect to accountability. Much depends, therefore, on the digital literacy of not only managers but also elected officials and the public at large.

At the same time, today's young adults—studying and seeking entry into the workforce—are categorically different in having never known a world without significant virtual dimensions According to Booz & Company, Generation C, those born after 1990 and destined to encompass roughly 40 % of the populations of North America and Europe by 2020, refers to an increasingly digitized youth segment that are "connected, communicating, content-centric, computerized, community oriented, and always clicking" (Roman et al. 2010). For many in this grouping, traditional boundaries between the workplace, education, socializing, and organizing have dissolved into a more seamless landscape blending physical and virtual dimensions in ways that align naturally with—and are indeed underpinned by—cloud-based infrastructures.

Although such depictions of a mobile generation are not universal, masking as they do both diversity in usage and ongoing digital divides in most all countries, they do apply to a growing proportion on young people in a manner that is consequential in two ways. Firstly, government finds itself under growing strain to ensure technological responsiveness and relevance to this more mobile and evermore connected generation (while also accommodating other segments of the citizenry unable or unwilling to embrace such practices).

Secondly and somewhat related, depictions of "Generation C" apply most obviously and accurately to the most educated and especially to those housed within postsecondary institutions as well as recent graduates—and it is this group that defines the professional cadre of tomorrow's public servants far less suited to the traditional values and traits of a governmental workforce, namely, hierarchical deference and anonymity. In Canada, already, a number of new movements led by public servants themselves have been formed in recent months and years in accordance with such trends. As one Canadian public servant argues

> public servants from different Departments and Agencies are actively contributing personal and professional time and effort to solve common problems and learn from one another. And this is regardless of the position they happen to occupy at the present time…or for any tangible rewards. (p. 11, Conabree 2011)

Nonetheless, within government, traditional structures and behaviors are difficult to modify, and this has certainly proved no different with respect to digital infrastructure since the advent of e-government (Fountain 2001; Kraemer and King 2005; Roy 2006, 2008; Fyfe and Crookall 2010). One study, for example, of senior managers within the Ontario Government found that they "have not acclimatized to the age of collaborative technologies and continue to use the tools in a Web 1.0 manner" (p. 117, Bermonte 2011). Yet the study also notes considerable experimentation and widening openness to novel approaches to decision-making and organization (ibid.). Such are the sorts of schisms and cleavages at the heart of tensions between machinery and mobility.

Meanwhile Back on the Ground

The tribulations of digital transformation for government are not new (Roy 2006; Dunleavy et al. 2006; Lips 2012). Yet an important irony of the emerging mobility era is that while smarter and smaller devices become easier and more intuitive to use for individuals, the organizational challenges facing the public sector in adapting to a shifting digital architecture arguably become more complex. This message lies at the heart of one of the OECD's earliest publications on e-government aptly titled *The Hidden Threat to E-Government*, which underscores how peril trumps promise unless the mundane details of procuring and managing IT systems are mastered (OECD 2001).

One decade later, a British Parliamentary Committee Report, *Recipe for Rip-Off*, exemplifies the salience of the OECD's warning and ongoing struggles in this regard. Among the culprits, the report identifies a number of important factors:

- Projects tended to be too big, leading to greater risk, complexity and limiting the range of suppliers who could compete;
- Departments, agencies, and public bodies too rarely reused and adapted systems available off the shelf or that had already been commissioned by another part of government, leading to wasteful duplication;
- Systems were too rarely interoperable;
- The infrastructure was insufficiently integrated, leading to inefficiency and separation;
- There was serious over-capacity, especially in data centers;
- Procurement timescales were far too long and costly, squeezing out all but the biggest suppliers; and
- There had been too little attention given at senior levels to the implementation of big ICT projects and programs, either by senior officials or by ministers. (p. 2, Public Administration Committee, British House of Commons 2011).

Similar sentiments can be found in many countries, including the United States, where the election of President Obama in 2008 promised to usher in a new era of digital renewal both politically and managerially (various facets of which are examined throughout this book). Championed by the first president to insist on using a Blackberry mobile device, several prominent officials were imported into the administration promising a radical overhaul of the federal government's IT infrastructure. Much like the president himself, his administration's newly chosen Chief Information Officer (CIO) found a daunting set of realities awaiting him:

On his first day at the White House, Kundra was greeted by staffers who, instead of carrying smart devices, handed him a pile of papers. "'Here's a stack of PDF documents about $27 billion of IT projects behind schedule,'" Kundra recalled them saying. When he asked the staffers why they didn't have mobile devices, they answered that such devices were passed out based on seniority, and that there was a long wait list to get one. "I first realized the challenges facing the nation," he said. (p. 1, Kovar 2011)

The advent of the cloud is thus viewed by many as an opportunity to forge a new mindset and to put in place a shared and more modular, efficient, and flexible infrastructure capable of modernizing the public sector and overcoming many of the pitfalls highlighted in the aforementioned British review. Yet some 3 years into the first Obama mandate, reality had set in. Obama's chosen Chief Information Officer (CIO) for the federal government departed for the private sector, no doubt worn down by the drudgery of attempting to realize large-scale transformation in an unrelentingly incremental and contested fashion. Kundra's evolution from a government CIO to private sector vendor underscores the centrality of procurement and industry relations, also a key theme of the British report.

Nevertheless, significant change has occurred in the American government over the past few years—in no small measure to Presidential interest and decree. Open data, cloud computing, social media and public engagement, cybersecurity, and mobility are all themes that received much attention in recent years, leading to some important initiatives, many examined in subsequent chapters. Yet both the American and British experiences underscore the immense difficulty of effectively embracing digital currents, both administratively and politically, a recurring theme throughout this book. Such difficulties also reflect wider societal tensions at play between openness and democracy, on the one hand, and secrecy and control on the other hand.

Mobility's Inherent Tensions

The mobility era builds upon preceding waves of online connectivity and virtual governance in surmounting the traditional logic of bureaucratic control as plummeting costs of organizing collectively coupled with plentiful information and tools for collaborating produce conditions that are ripe for networks (Tapscott and Williams 2006; Shirky 2008; Roy 2008; Dutil et al. 2010; Reddick and Aikins 2012). As trust becomes evermore contested across more informed and better educated cadres of citizens, managers, entrepreneurs, and activists, it enjoins itself with an infrastructure and mindset of mobility that calls into question both the legitimacy and utility of formal organizing structures. Accordingly, Shirky's aptly titled book, "Here Comes Everybody: The Power of Organizing Without Organizations," offers a window on a world facilitated by plummeting coordinating costs, on the one hand, and vastly expanding opportunities for networking on the other hand (Shirky 2008).[3]

The facilitation and leveraging of a more agile and engaging public sector are central to a more collaborative ethos for society as a whole. One such optimistic vantage point is well articulated by Accenture Consulting—a value shift to social prosperity brought about through ubiquitous Internet access and new patterns of more networked and collective intelligence that emerge:

> Cooperation, diversity, openness and sharing of knowledge will not only have a dramatic effect on the economy, but also on society as a whole...People decide to make use of their collective intelligence, build networks and organize their community activities by themselves. This approach toward collective social prosperity fosters new ways of thinking and dealing with information and intellectual property. (p. 4, Accenture 2009)

Such a context becomes a recipe for Shirky's more organic and adaptive forms of governance leveraging these new social and technological conditions. Yet within government, as noted, it is often engrained methodologies, rules, and norms in dealing with information and intellectual property that most often prevail—a point well illustrated by a 2011 review of IT governance by a British Parliamentary Committee highlighted above (Public Administration Committee 2011).

---

[3] Indeed, an early tale of the tracing a lost smartphone in the opening to this book closely resembles the example referenced in the preface of this book.

Such tensions also apply to organizations and societies more widely: historical research on the impacts of IT on organizations shows its impacts to most often be incremental rather than revolutionary, viewed and deployed by those with power as a means to maintain and deepen it (Kraemer and King 2005). Shirky's pronouncements about social media's democratizing impacts around the world were similarly gradual and cautious in this regard, emphasizing that the democratization of information for societies at large could not, overnight, transform the structures of state power—particularly in lesser and anti-democratic regimes (Shirky 2011). Yet recent events in the Middle East, notably Tunisia and Egypt, seemed to greatly accelerate such timelines, illuminating tensions between demands for openness and change and equally prevalent gravitational pressures for stability and control.

As Egyptian protestors so readily and effectively mobilized in the spring of 2011, it is only appropriate that Google featured prominently. One of the leading figures in the protests was himself a former Google employee, and the widespread usage of this company's infrastructure and tools among other prominent social media platforms such as Facebook and Twitter (to name the most prominent) facilitated a social movement (dubbed Revolution 2.0) that quickly grew to overtake efforts by authorities to muzzle and contain the fledging movement.

Nevertheless, the decentralized and informal governance of those inhabiting Tahrir Square would also prove to be limiting and insufficient in ushering forward changes and the creation of a new political regime (and such tensions vividly displayed themselves throughout the 2012 struggles of a Presidential election and subsequent formation of a new constitution). Despite this real potential for collective innovation from newly derived strengths of widened networks, others suggest that this strength of weak ties also carries limits. Previewing the struggles of Egyptians to create a new and more democratic political regime, Gladwell argues that social media is insufficient for large-scale systemic change:

> The drawbacks of networks scarcely matter if the network isn't interested in systemic change—if it just wants to frighten or humiliate or make a splash—or if it doesn't need to think strategically. But if you're taking on a powerful and organized establishment you have to be a hierarchy. (p. 1, Gladwell 2010)

In 2012, therefore, both Egypt and Mexico featured widening societal demands for democracy (with urbanized and tech-savvy youth movements prominent in both countries) and national elections that ultimately delivered heightened degrees of centralizing authority for newly elected leaders (and serious questions in and about both countries pertaining to the sustainability of a democratic political regime). The expansion of mobility strengthens conditions for more widespread participation and collaboration. Yet within political and administrative contexts, such conditions must be aligned with formal hierarchical processes stemming from traditional notions of political legitimacy and like-minded models of accountability.

While more dramatically illustrated in societies undergoing or attempting to engineer fundamental political transformation, such tensions are equally prevalent within existing democracies as well. In both Canada and the US, political parties and evolving electoral tactics lie at the heart of a social media paradox—espousing greater democratization to both partisan members and society more widely yet increasingly centralized with respect to operational governance and strategic conduct (Roy 2012a). Despite new media's widespread promise to "join the conversation" and political pledges for online engagement, politics in general—and most especially formal electoral contests—become more fractious and divisive and dictated by the messaging of highly contained and centrally managed partisan vessels (Shane 2004; Owens 2010; Pole 2011).

A cursory review of social media usage by the Canadian public sector illustrates this point and the repercussions for the mindset and actions of those in public office having secured an electoral mandate in such a manner. Despite the presence on social media venues of many politicians from all political parties, the official websites of the legislative branch (i.e., the Canadian Parliament) are devoid of any social media channels and links. By contrast, the executive branch (led by the Prime Minister and his Conservative Party) includes an array of social media tools mostly all designed to communicate information and imaging on government policies and services. Such pronouncements are typically fashioned in a partisan manner, highlighting Ministerial action and above all else the branding of the "Harper Government."[4]

Accordingly, the Prime Minister dominates in the realm of Twitter—of course less a reflection of continual tweeting on the part of the individual himself than a sophisticated partisan and communications-oriented apparatus designed to both proactively and reactively shape both image and message. Echoing long-standing concerns about Prime Ministerial dominance that predate but are seemingly accelerated by online visibility and interaction, Prime Minister Harper has nearly twice as many Twitter followers as the next most "popular" Member of Parliament (though still a tiny proportion of the overall population).

Perhaps more telling is the reality that of more than 300 elected members of Parliament, only two can boast to having more than 100,000 followers (throughout 2012), a modest number in a country with more than 30 million people (and in 2011 the highest proportion of this populous anywhere in the world engaged in social media). Despite many surveys demonstrating a widespread desire across the Canadian populous for social media to serve as a platform of engagement with elected officials,[5] the overwhelming usage of social media channels such as Facebook and Twitter at present is broadcast oriented with little in the way of

---

[4] See http://www.gc.ca for the main Government of Canada homepage.

[5] For example, a 2011 Fleishman-Hillard public engagement survey "revealed that Canadians would be more engaged in conversations on government policy if there were ways to participate online. The same study also revealed that a third of Canadians have an improved view of elected officials who use social media to engage with constituents." *Source*: http://www.newswire.ca/en/story/848851/social-media-key-to-citizen-engagement-54-of-canadians-would-engage-more-with-government-if-there-were-ways-to-participate-online

substantive exchange.[6] Indeed, it is telling in this regard that the official Government of Canada website devoted to public consultation exercises is completely devoid of social media tools and channels.[7]

At the same time, beyond partisan branding and media messaging, Prime Ministers and Ministers must also defend themselves in this new and often confrontational electronic arena—in ways that are reshaping the boundaries between personal and public. The recent introduction by the Canadian Government of controversial legislation to augment government surveillance capacities over Internet traffic led to the Minister responsible for the proposals being subject to online disclosure of highly personal details of his recent divorce proceedings and settlement.

The perpetrator was exposed as a partisan operative of an opposition Party and the leader of that Party issued an eloquent apology in Parliament, yet the incident led to wider concerns about how other Parliamentarians reacted and made usage of this information in online tweets and postings. According to one media commentator of a prominent online venue, such is the new norm in today's shifting political environment where social media accentuates the most confrontational dynamics of previous eras and delivers enhanced and unrelenting transparency in a manner akin to the expectations and conduct of today's social media generation:

> Politicians stand in the House all the time and attack each other's intelligence; pundits go on TV and spin us dizzy; parties blanket ridings in push polls at the taxpayers' expense. For the most part, we allow these acts to not only go unpunished, but to be celebrated. We're kicking ass in politics! Here's how you win elections, guys!

> The Facebook generation is just taking that message and adapting it to our own bag of tricks. Say hello to the political operatives of tomorrow: cyber bullies, anonymous bloggers and internet trolls. Love them like you would love your children, because they were raised in your image.

> Get used to this style of politics. The Facebook generation—already accustomed to full disclosure—just had their political coming out party. Welcome them to the game; they're just taking their cues from those who came first (p.1, Owens 2012).

This viewpoint illustrates the aforementioned tensions accentuated by the mobility era. Despite a broadly democratized society—in terms of education, online access, and political awareness— the expansion and usage of social media threaten to be more fragmenting than unifying. On the one hand, it is a highly engaged minority of observers and activists—for whom social media is the next frontier of partisan battles demanding centralized and disciplined messaging. On the other hand, despite this heightened visibility, political parties and politics more generally are suffering an erosion of civic involvement and rising levels of indifference, cynicism,

---

[6]On a 2011 visit to China, for example, the Prime Minister tweeted of his encounter with a Panda Bear at a Chinese zoo (though somewhat unfairly antidotal, such an example is indicative of the sorts of tweets often coming from politicians seeking to increase familiarity and personal appeal with the public).

[7]This characterization is true through to the end of 2012: http://www.consultingcanadians.gc.ca/cpcPubHome.jsp?lang=en

and exclusion in part due to the cleavage between a more empowered and participatory society and a more scripted, constrained, and centralized electoral and political culture (Roy 2011).

Research in the US reveals a similar evolution. One study of the 2010 Congressional election cycle, for example, found that growing portions of the public utilized the Internet as a means of becoming politically informed—but also recognized that in doing so, they were more likely to be seeking out viewpoints similar to their own (Smith 2011). The 2012 Presidential election accentuated such findings, with many viewing "politics" as a term of disrepute (MacGallis 2012). Correspondingly, the Obama campaign in 2012 became more digitized than in 2008; yet the emphasis shifted from grassroots engagement and building communities of support to data-mining and messaging operations designed to dissect the electorate and target specified (i.e., most likely to be supportive) voters on issues and themes deemed most relevant and appealing.

Machinery Vs. Mobility

The resulting democratic and administrative context for public sector experimentation and adaptation with respect to new forms of digital infrastructure and heightened mobility is contradictory in many important respects. The consequences are profound for public servants, elected officials, and citizens alike, much as their respective roles and interrelationships are impacted and evermore fluid.

On the one hand, there is empowerment and democratization writ large. In recent years, Web 2.0 has emerged as a proxy not only for new technological capacities but also for a new social paradigm with sweeping implications for all sectors. In contrast to static web pages where users are recipients of information, Web 2.0 denotes a more interactive and participatory version of the Internet where content is created and shared more organically and openly. Collaboration is the critical lubricant of Web 2.0 as an evolving and more interactive online architecture, an emerging "age of participation" viewed as an historical occasion to fundamentally rethink how governments interact and engage with their citizens, greatly expanding opportunities for public engagement and involvement in governance design and execution (Flumian 2009; Meijer 2011; Dutil et al. 2010).

On the other hand, there is control and centralization. Under siege from a more informed and mobilized citizenry, many governments and their political leaders struggle to communicate their message. Tensions between proprietary software and hardware–and open-sourced variants—go far beyond the realm of technological design: they are at the heart of the contradictory forces at play within many governmental systems—including democracies such as Canada, where information secrecy and control are the predominant traditions in an era where transparency and collaboration are evermore widely espoused. Yet control remains the hallmark of government organization and accountability (Roy 2006, 2008).

Due to such countervailing currents, the purpose of this book is to dissect and better understand what lies ahead for democratic governance. In doing so, we dissect the main tensions between the political and administrative foundations of the traditional state apparatus, commonly referred to as the "machinery of government" within the Westminster Parliamentary lexicon, and alternative governance models and mindsets emerging due to the advent of the Internet and most recent emergence of the mobility era.

This book thus sets out to examine the roots and implications of the tensions between machinery and mobility both internally within public sector institutions and externally in terms of interactions with stakeholders and the citizenry. Furthermore, by examining how governments are wrestling with such tensions today, we aim to provide some underlying guidance and insights into the sorts of public sector reforms emerging today as well as those potentially on the horizon, both administratively and democratically.

A key presumption of this book is that politics and management are and must be viewed as closely interrelated, and one of the growing challenges of the mobility era is the fluidity of role and interrelationships of elected officials, public servants, and the citizenry. While this book is undertaken primarily from public administration and technology management vantage points, the inclusion of political and organizational perspectives is also warranted.

A central and guiding premise of this project is that the twin foundations of representational democracy and bureaucratic management (enjoined by a mindset of hierarchical and informational control, i.e., machinery) are increasingly out of step with the realities of today's digitally and socially networked era (mobility).

This book explains why this is so, the resulting impacts at present, and the consequences and choices that lie ahead.

Canada is a useful laboratory as a starting point and primary focus jurisdictionally: in 2011, it could claim status as the country with the greatest proportions of its citizenry embracing social media (a title it was nonetheless expected to relinquish to the US by 2012 based upon recent trends),[8] further building upon a preceding decade of e-government leadership (according to many global rankings undertaken by the likes of the United Nations and Accenture Consulting). Indeed, the globalizing nature of the Internet and virtual life underpins the many commonalities and shared lessons across jurisdictions: a wider lens of public sector strategies and experiences is thus warranted (Weerakkody and Reddick 2011; Ubaldi 2011; Reddick and Aikins 2012).

Examples are thus drawn from a number of OECD countries—notably those of Europe, Australia, and the neighboring US: the aforementioned digital impetus of President Obama provides an important reference point for many facets of Canadian

---

[8] In 2011, Canada had the most social networking users in the world on a per capita basis, according to research firm eMarketer. About 47.4 % of Canadians were using social media at least once a month in 2011, compared to 47.2 % of Americans, 42.4 % of South Koreans, and 40.2 % of Australians. As noted, Canada is expected to be overtaken by the US in 2012 using this same measurement basis (Oliveira 2012).

public sector governance. Furthermore, contrasts between national and local examples underscore a prevailing set of contradictory tendencies embedded in classic, territorial-based federalism of the sort characterizing countries such as Canada, the US, and Australia (Roy 2006; Ubaldi and Roy 2010). Whereas local governments may enjoy additional flexibility to innovate—both administratively and democratically—they are creatures legally subordinate to higher order governments whose fiscal capacities and digital visibility (across both traditional and social media spheres) often eclipse more localized governance processes and venues. This book thus draws upon examples and research from all levels of government—with contrasting national and local initiatives an important and recurring theme.

Within such wide parameters, the empirical evidence gathered for this undertaking is primarily Canadian, derived from conversations and interactions with hundreds of current and prospective public servants—as well as industry representatives and elected officials. In addition, this book provides an additional layering of previously related undertakings in the realm of digital government and networked governance (Roy 2006, 2008; Dutil et al. 2010; Ubaldi and Roy 2010; Lane and Roy 2011; Roy 2012a, b, c; Roy 2013).

Overview of Chapters

In dissecting the broad and diverse set of tensions between machinery and mobility impacting governments, the following is a brief synopsis of the main focus of each chapter that follows:

Chapter 2 delves within the public sector, exploring its conceptual foundations. The centrality of bureaucratic organization and secrecy is explored and explained and subsequently contrasted to today's more networked and collaborative governance patterns. Three conceptual schools of thought in terms of public sector organization and accountability shall be compared and contrasted in this regard: traditional public administration (emphasizing control), new public management (emphasizing competition), and public value management (emphasizing collaboration). This latter perspective, public value management, is most widely developed in the British public administration community, its emphasis on openness, networking, and engagement closely aligning with many aspects of so-called Web 2.0 governance models.

Chapter 3 examines how the spatial and cognitive organization of work and managerial authority is undergoing profound shifts in a world of connectivity and mobility. The notion of a more flexible and responsive work environment shall be examined along with offsetting challenges pertaining to information overload and the emergence of more complex organizational governance regimes within and extending outside of the public sector. Tensions between physicality and more virtual patterns of working and organizing are also examined as key dimensions to public sector efforts to become more mobile.

Chapter 4 reviews the basis for open-sourced government in terms of information creation, processing and sharing, and ownership, as well as tensions between traditional proprietary models of IT systems and the advent of open-sourced solutions. The advent of open data and apps for democracy and government shall be explored, drawing upon specific initiatives undertaken by governments in Canada and elsewhere. Within this dynamic technological and governance setting, the consequences for public sector entities are examined with respect to procurement and performance.

Chapter 5 presents the multifaceted challenge of cybersecurity for a public sector more open and increasingly reliant on cloud-based infrastructure, social media platforms, and networked infrastructures. Drawing primarily from US efforts under President Obama, tensions between secrecy and openness and between bureaucratic and more flexible and organic governance capacities are explored. In addition, the behavioral ethos of an online world is examined from the public's perspective—including both customer and citizenship dimensions to such an ethos as well as the implications for individual privacy and collective security.

Chapter 6 addresses the closely related concepts of privacy and payments—the former an important issue in the preceding discussions of openness, cloud computing, and cybersecurity, and the latter a widening focus of government and industry in most all developed countries. Payment reform is particularly relevant in light of the emphasis on paperless and electronic service delivery by public sector authorities along with new pressures for mobile payment options enjoining various industries, government, and smartphone-laden societies. The implications for and contrasts between customer and citizen dimensions to personal conduct and information and identity safety are also examined.

The focus of Chap. 7 is the widening canvas of public engagement in an increasingly virtual and mobile world and corresponding pressures and efforts to rethink the balance between traditional representational models of democracy and more direct and participative mechanisms for public involvement. The advent of electronic democracy (e-democracy) and the central importance of social media are examined—along with the deliberative challenge in a political and media environment arguably more suited to adversarial exchange than thoughtful reflection and collective learning. In accordance with mobility, the emergence of open-source democracy is discussed.

Building on these themes, Chap. 8 situates the development of such a renewed ethos within the administrative and political realities of global financial uncertainty and corresponding budgetary processes by governments—particularly at the national level. Furthermore, related tensions between national governance systems and intergovernmental and federalist dynamics are also examined, especially prevalent in light of the localizing flavor of democratic experimentation in Chap. 7. Within such fiscal and federalist contexts, the recent digital initiatives of the Government of Canada are examined along with present prospects for realizing more mobility-laden governance capacities.

Finally, the book's conclusion draws together the key lessons learned from the preceding chapters into a forward-looking template summarized by the acronym V.O.I.C.E. (each letter encapsulating elements of both change and resistance in wrestling with tensions between machinery and mobility). Building upon this better understanding of these critical tension points, the book further concludes with a discussion of the sorts of cultural and procedural directions for collectively renewing the organization and conduct of the public sector for a more mobile and participative era.

Having shed some light on both opportunities and pitfalls in this regard, this book ultimately aims to provide some of the groundwork for cultivating more open, innovative, and collaborative modes of democratic governance.

Chapter 2
Bureaucracy Versus Mobility

S.O.C.I.A.L. Governance

In late 2011, New York Times columnist, Thomas Freidman, described the convergence of cloud computing, social media, and mobile technologies as the basis of a revolution in governance, giving rise to what one leading industry figure had termed, S.O.C.I.A.L., an acronym for the sorts of changes underway: S, Speed; O, Open; C, Collaboration; I, Individual; A, Alignment; and L, Leadership (Freidman 2011).

Freidman added that in a "social" world, leadership must be both top–down and bottom–up in order to inspire, enable, and empower—the latter a particularly central and pervasive theme to the positive leveraging of social media both within the workplace and externally. Batorski and Hadden (2010) echo the importance of a paradigm shift in leadership as an essential enabler of effective organizational change and value creation in government:

> Web 2.0 brings with it a swift pace of change that requires organizational leaders to adopt new ways of thinking and new behaviours (Kobza 2008). Leading change in the Government 2.0 era requires new leadership skills that include listening, influencing, collaborating, and stakeholder inclusion…The key difference in the era of Government 2.0 for leaders is in the need to engage with others, to convert value from the network into meaningful products and services and knowledge, and to identify practical solutions to challenges. (p. 3, Batorski and Hadden 2010)

New forms of collaborative and open leadership are becoming an imperative as an increasingly networked and online society takes hold. Yet, as already noted, the political contours of political life in a digital world are often centralizing in many respects, constraining the emergence and traction of new forms of leadership and new governance models.

Whereas mobility promotes and personifies openness and networks—the sort of "social" environment of which Freidman and others speak—the political and organizational foundations of the "machinery" of government are secrecy and bureaucracy. Understanding this clash is central to dissecting the challenges faced by the public sector today—a precursor to orchestrating any adaptation that must

J. Roy, *From Machinery to Mobility: Government and Democracy in a Participative Age*,
Public Administration and Information Technology 2, DOI 10.1007/978-1-4614-7221-6_2,
© Springer Science+Business Media New York 2013

find ways to refurbish rather than abandon traditional public sector underpinnings with respect to behavioral values and culture and organizational and political structures.

Bureaucratic Foundations of Government

The stability and functionality of the Westminster model of Parliamentary government (in use across the Commonwealth with variants of Parliamentary governance found in much of Europe and parts of Asia) are dependent upon three central, relational compacts: firstly, representative democracy as the compact between the public and elected officials (Parliamentarians); secondly, ministerial accountability as the compact between elected officials and the government on the one hand and the appointed public service on the other hand; and, thirdly, loyalty and hierarchy as the main value and chief organizing principle within the public service for assuring that government plans and policies are executed and implemented (Roy 2008).

The third point has traditionally served as the central pillar of bureaucratic organization within the public sector. An anonymous and quasi-permanent public servant (shielded from direct public scrutiny and answerability and safeguarded by protections and expectations of political neutrality) advises and executes on demand while remaining by and large deferential to Ministerial prerogative and direction. The extent to which any discretionary empowerment of the public service takes place according to strictly traditional customs is a matter solely for determination by Ministers individually and collectively (ibid.).

The 2011 case of Statistics Canada and the national census bears this out. Despite some limited legislative autonomy (distinguishing it from a classic line department) and a tradition over past decades of an arm's length operational role from government (viewed as essential to an objective role in gathering and analyzing information), The Government would ultimately reject the agency's advice against the abandonment of a mandatory, long-form census (viewed as essential by the agency for a sufficiently robust sample of the population). The fact that the Departmental Head of Statistics Canada would eventually speak out publicly to clarify his technical advice and views on the policy change was interpreted by politicians and the media alike as an extraordinary act of defiance (and thus accompanied by resignation), contrary to the bureaucracy's traditionally deferential role to the preeminence of elected officials.

While the Westminster Parliamentary model is uniquely inward and centralizing in terms of a role for the public service, the prevalence of bureaucratic structures and mindsets within government is commonplace. In the US, for example, a much more politicized public service of Presidential appointees reflects the Congressional role in both passing legislation and formally scrutinizing administrative plans and actions: a more frontline and visible role for public servants thus ensues. Nonetheless, while some public servants are political appointees—reflecting this duality of legislative authority across the Presidential and Congressional dimensions of government—the bulk of public staff remain unchanged through election cycles, and the importance of hierarchy and deference to elected officials (albeit multiple sets of elected officials) remains, not unlike the Westminster model in this regard.

Indeed, within the US public sector model, the overriding patterns of vertical silos were most acutely exposed in the aftermath of 9–11; the inability of government agencies to collaborate became a sudden strategic imperative that, though less dramatically, also became a central concern in early e-government efforts to forge interoperable and integrative service delivery efforts (Fountain 2001; Kamarck 2002; Roy 2006). Tellingly, the initial response to 9–11 featured a massive bureaucratic consolidation of agencies and authority within a more unified chain of command (the Department of Homeland Security reporting to its new Presidential appointee), though in more recent years a more nuanced debate has emerged with respect to realizing cross-governmental networks and more flexible governance capacities (the case of cybersecurity is examined in some detail in Chap. 5).

Across other Westminster jurisdictions, we also see efforts to stretch and reform the traditional model and attempt to more formally recognize the roles and plurality of accountabilities that define the workings of the public service (Roy 2008). At the dusk of the twentieth century, such efforts most often centered on market-inspired prescriptions—the basis of new public management and its main tenants that were often pursued in distinct and different ways across jurisdictions. Such reforms generally have included (1) outsourcing government functions or segments of government operations to the private sector; (2) infusing the state sector with business-inspired models more decentralized, autonomous, and focused on outcomes (with a primordial concern for efficiency); and (3), most recently and remaining very much intertwined with digital government efforts, an importation of a customer service mentality into the delivery apparatus of the public sector (Dutil et al. 2010).

For government managers, the thrust of new public management is to lessen bureaucracy rather than banish it—creating an environment where smaller units of government would face competitive pressures and incentives to act more efficiently and in manners more predicated measuring and improving performance than respecting process. New public management would play an important role in terms of e-government's early emergence as a primarily service-driven reform agenda (from the point of view of government), on the one hand, and in terms of seeking greater industry involvement in IT refurbishment on the other hand. In Canada, for instance, early service transformation vehicles across many provincial jurisdictions featured newly empowered and autonomous agencies created to act more "business like," often partnering with industry to devise mechanisms and processes for online service delivery and back-end integrative processes (ibid.).

One example is Service New Brunswick (SNB), a model that partially paved the way for the creation of Service Canada federally: SNB's autonomy as a provincial crown corporation facilitated a more business-like approach and the formation of unique public-private partnerships (ibid.). Similarly, the most successful federal agency processing online services—the Canada Revenue Agency—had been previously transformed from a traditional department into an operationally autonomous agency precisely to add a dose of NPM-inspired flexibility and innovation that would prove effective in championing online tax services (ibid.).

Nonetheless, new public management would also encounter important limitations and blockages as e-government took hold, due to pressures for interoperability and more cross-governmental coordination that lead to more recent and centralizing tendencies. In jurisdictions such as Canada which had not shifted far from the traditional Westminster model (unlike, e.g., New Zealand), centralizing political and bureaucratic mindsets remained deeply engrained, readily able to reassert themselves as circumstances warranted. During the previous decade, moreover, a significant federal government scandal involving mismanagement of spending (the so-called sponsorship scandal) would provide fertile ground for advocates of more centralized and bolstered bureaucratic oversight from central agencies (Clark and Swain 2005), reinforcing the vertical segmentation of individualized units less flexible and autonomous to act in their one manner and in concert with one another. The stunted evolution of Service Canada—once envisioned as an autonomous service integrator for the federal government as a whole (akin to SNB provincially) but never having fostered the horizontal governance capacities necessary to do so— illustrates such tensions and the inertia of traditionalism (Flumian et al. 2007; Belanger et al. 2007; Roy 2012b).

Secrecy and Control

Centralizing forces in government also owe much to the interplay of democratic processes and bureaucratic structures initially created and still more suited for a world of information scarcity rather than abundance: in other words information management as primarily about control (Roberts 2006). A parallel of sorts has emerged over the past two decades between the emergence of e-government and rhetoric of wider transparency on the one hand, and augmenting charges against provincial and federal governments in Canada in terms of endemic secrecy on the other hand (Roy 2006, 2008, 2012b). These seemingly contradictory forces are the result of governments embracing the Internet as a platform for openness in specifically controlled ways–especially in terms of service provision, while resisting other demands and opportunities for transparency that for one reason or another may appear threatening or destabilizing (Reddick and Aikins 2012).

Foundational for democratic governance of any form, the importance of openness has been articulated in a decision of the Supreme Court of Canada in 1997:

> The overarching purpose of access to information legislation…is to facilitate democracy. It does so in two related ways. It helps to ensure, first, that citizens have the information required to participate meaningfully in the democratic process and secondly, that politicians and bureaucrats remain accountable to the citizenry. (p. 80, Reid 2004)

Although there is no standardized definition of what it means for the public sector to be transparent, a useful starting point is to equate transparency with some degree of openness to those with either a right or an expectation of being able to scrutinize and understand government decision-making and policy action. Transparency thus underpins accountability, and the emergence of the Internet has heightened expectation for more government transparency as an informationally empowered citizenry alters its views on authority and power, shunning deference and attaching far less importance to traditional representational roles and structures (McNutt 2009; Roy 2010, 2011, 2012c).

Here lies a major foundational shift for power relations and democratic governance. A world of information scarcity is one that is highly conducive to bureaucratic power and organizational secrecy within the state (central elements of the Westminster model) and representational democracy outside of it (Roy 2008, 2012a). A world of mobility, by contrast, is far less conducive to both hierarchical control and information secrecy.

Reliance on secrecy begins at the apex of power, where Cabinet meets in the closed confines of a forum designed to contain but also paradoxically share information and insight. Secrecy was originally viewed as a means to facilitate open deliberation among Ministers in order to generate consensus on actions and policies that, in turn, would be presented to Parliament for further debate prior to legislative adoption—often in modified form. As Savoie and others have aptly demonstrated, Cabinet secrecy has since become less deliberative and more dictated by Prime Ministerial direction (as policy debates previously housed in Cabinet have since been dispersed across numerous venues both inside and outside of government). Key to this evolution is the desire to package decisions for subsequent communication—not to Parliament but rather directly to the electorate as a whole. Parliament's role is thus greatly diminished (Aucoin et al. 2011; Savoie 1999).

With Parliament viewed as less relevant (and more adversarial) and external points of scrutiny and influence multiplying, Cabinet secrecy has become more pervasive (much like the usage of Executive Privilege within the Presidential model) despite escalating challenges and costs in preserving such a cloak. The result is a systemic culture engrained in the executive branch predicated on the presumption that information must be contained and managed (Roberts 2006). Ironically, online channels—often viewed as drivers of transparency—may well be leveraged primarily by governments in power as new tools to convey and spin partisan messages (as described in the introduction and a theme returned to in later chapters).

Such is the schizophrenia displayed in the UK where the Blair Government was credited with both introducing the country's first comprehensive access to information law (in 2005) while forging a sophisticated communications and media relations apparatus viewed as aggressive and often manipulative in shaping and limiting such openness (Roberts 2006). Indeed, Blair would later reflect on such legislation as one of his worst mistakes (due to its cyclical impacts of media suspicion and exposure, government defensiveness, and public cynicism).[1] Similarly contrasting

---

[1]These sorts of struggles have continued unabated through successive Labour and Coalition Governments cresting with 2011 scandals involving phone-tapping by various media outlets and close relationship between the Murdoch media empire and political officials (leading to a formal public inquiry in 2012).

portraits of Prime Minister Harper reveal similar pledges before taking office to pursue greater systemic openness, some initial legislative steps in such a direction, and subsequent regressions into defensive secrecy and centralizing efforts to contain information and shape messaging (Martin 2010).

In short, the Internet's explosion of information and mobilization externally has also fueled a reinforcement of hierarchy and control internally—due to the powerful inertia of traditional structures and culture of government. Bureaucracy is thus both challenged and fortified, often simultaneously. The steady expansion of Web 2.0, mobility, and "social" governance trends (to return to Freidman's terminology at the outset of the chapter) nonetheless strengthens the case for an alternative governance ethos—rooted in contrasting first principles and realities.

An Alternative Governance Ethos

With respect to crafting an alternate prism to bureaucratic machinery, Thomas (2008) provides a useful starting point in contrasting "government" with "governance":

> Government has become increasingly centralized, vertical and personalized through the focus on the person and the office of the Prime Minister…Governance is a related, but wider process than government. It involves sweeping, impersonal forces of economic, technological, social and political change. Governance involves dispersed, connective and shared leadership operating through decentralized shifting, networked relations.
>
> The tensions between centralized government and decentralized governance are heightened by the public mood of mistrust and weak confidence in governments. This fundamental shift towards governance from the traditional processes of government has numerous implications for the future role of the public service, many of which cannot be clearly foreseen at this point. (p. 4, Thomas 2008)

In terms of a "government" ethos, then, as Thomas indicates what we typically see within Parliamentary democracies is the traditional Westminster doctrine of administration and democracy that places the emphasis squarely on control and communication. By contrast, within an emerging mobility context—where Web 2.0 denotes a set of technological, social, and organizational forces—the premium is placed upon collaboration, participation, and consultation (much more about governance in Thomas's depiction above).

This alternate post-bureaucratic ethos interwoven with mobility (and underpinning calls for "Government 2.0" though in line with Thomas's notion of "governance") is driven by a massive expansion of the means to both produce and share information and knowledge. This knowledge, and the shared learning, that results is an important component of service design and effective delivery in a world of mass collaboration and distributed governance models (Flumian 2009; Dutil et al. 2010; Meijer 2011).

Even as Thomas's depiction captures much of the essence of today's governance dichotomy between traditional and new, many of its elements in the latter realm have long been recognized as important attributes in overcoming the limitations of bureaucratic specialization and hierarchical control. For instance, the centrality of learning, greatly unleashed by the power of mobility and collective intelligence, has long been viewed as a critical determinant of governance resilience for organizations and societies alike. Schon puts it well:

> We must... become adept at learning. We must become able not only to transform our institutions, in response to changing situations and requirements; we must invent and develop institutions [and societies] that are "learning systems," that is to say, systems capable of bringing about their own continuing transformation. (p. 30, Schon 1971)

With respect to the public sector and a more networked canvass of public, private, and civic actors, Paquet's notions of the "strategic state" and "distributed governance" point to new and more collaborative directions very much post-bureaucratic in culture and form (Paquet 1997, 2004). A stable state is bureaucratic, whereas a strategic state is adept at adaption and navigation in less certain and more contested surroundings. Public servant must thus become able to orchestrate conditions for learning and engagement and the sort of continual transformation sought by Schon and others like him (Hubbard et al. 2012).

Seeking to move beyond bureaucratic rigidity on the one hand and the market and competitive doctrine of new public management on the other hand, British theorists have instead turned to public value management (PVM) as a governance prism better suited to more complexity, collaboration, and consultation both within and outside of government. Stoker describes the essence of PVM, in contrast to traditional public administration and new public management, as one which creates new sets of expectations for a more empowered, consultative, and discursive public servant outwardly engaged in a complex environment:

> Unlike the creation of value in the private sector, public value has no bottom line, so in the 'Government world' the creation of public value needs to be assessed through the collective democratic processes and dialogue between citizens, politicians and managers about what is provided at what cost.
>
> ...the idea of public value management is posited as an alternative to and development from NPM with the latter's narrow focus on squeezing out inefficiency and meeting performance targets. The public value framework reflects a desire to move on from a sterile debate between dichotomous views of public bureaucracy as either passive and responsive, as in a hierarchical commissioning environment, or self-interested and therefore in need of quasi market disciplines to ensure efficient delivery.
>
> ...The ability of public managers to anchor, or broker, a conversation between citizens and politicians in order to ensure efficient, appropriate and innovatory public service provision is taking place in a more complicated delivery environment. In particular, four developments are identified which impact upon the ability of public managers to follow a public value approach: the pluralism of policy advice, overlapping accountabilities, greater pressure to deliver and complex patterns of vertical integration in governance. (p. 6, Stoker 2005)

Within bureaucratic settings, collaborative and learning strategies designed to improve internal decision-making often featured tools and information systems that created prospectively shared platforms for shared decision-making. Such efforts often characterized, for instance, the initial phases of e-government in attempting to bundle services across previously separate agencies and departments, often with mixed results (Roy 2006; Borins et al. 2007; McNutt and Carey 2008; Reddick 2011; Roy 2013; Reddick and Roy 2013). Without a sense of community and engagement, however, such platforms cannot be harnessed into sources of collective innovation and shared governance.

As one senior Australian public servant frames it, organizational capabilities must be modular, scalable, and shared, accompanied by efforts for "the removal of barriers and the creation of the behavioral systems, symbols, skills and structures in our organizations that will enable successful collaboration, strong networks and stronger communities" (p. 6, Treadwell 2007). Examining the emergence of precisely these sorts of new capabilities in New Zealand (as well as more widely), Lips articulates a basis for "public administration 2.0" that seeks to align the complexities of technological design with fluid and collaborative administrative and political realities consistent with the advent of PVM (Lips 2012).

Accordingly and central to the argumentation of this book, mobility and the emergence of more participative governance schemes, such as those described here, are premised on a preference and indeed necessity for empowerment rather than containment and bureaucracy's penchant for control.

The resulting emphasis on complexity and chaordic governance arrangements facilitated by learning and adaptation suggests a public sector less controlled from the center (both politically and centrally). The former Canadian Deputy Minister responsible for the creation of Service Canada recognizes this logic, characterizing a shift from viewing and treating the public as customers via a mass production (and mainly transactional) paradigm to one that views the public as "prosumers" more directly engaged in service design via open and collaborative communities (termed ecosystems):

> Traditionally, governments design services and roll them out to citizens who are expected to comply with the terms and conditions of a program. Typically, the service is the same for everyone. It is always linear. Outputs are the metrics for the model: how many cheques got in the mail, how many people got back to work, how many calls got answered. Compliance with the service design's rules and regulations is paramount, especially in transactional services.
>
> The new model of service is not a mass production machine. Instead, in a more holistic fashion, service is directly connected to outcomes. Enabled by powerful information systems and ongoing interactions that help build a profound understanding of service needs, service providers and service users collaborate to creating services together. They use the 'information ecosystem' created by Web 2.0 technologies to re-calibrate the relationship between service providers, service users and the evidence of service outcomes. Information fuels collaboration on the way to achieving a goal. (p. 10, Flumian 2009)

This alternative depiction of governance—more bottom–up, learning driven, collaborative, and networked—fits well with today's digitally and socially networked landscape. In terms of government, however, such forces are novel and often contrary to the more historically embedded bureaucratic foundations premised upon hierarchical leadership and information control. It is, therefore, useful to examine how such counterforces are also to be found in typically younger governance models of private sector companies driving technological change and the advent of the mobility paradigm.

Google, Facebook, and Familiar Tensions

In North America, Apple, Google, Facebook, and Research in Motion (RIM) have all faced related tensions in balancing a relentless emphasis on innovation and collaboration with strong and centralized leadership. While RIM revamped its corporate governance regime and Apple has taken modest steps to increase shareholder democracy, Facebook is viewed by some as potentially overly centralized around the directive control of its founding CEO (Carmody 2012).

The specificities of each example notwithstanding, two profoundly important differences distinguish the organization and conduct of technology companies and those of governments. Firstly, internally, such companies have been recently created from anew in an organizational and social environment (i.e., Silicon Valley[2]) that largely shuns hierarchy and embraces flexibility and workplace empowerment as its starting point. Even alongside highly concentrated leadership at the apex of such organizations, governance arrangements are much more fluid and novel than what is typically found in government where traditions of control and risk averseness run deep. Moreover, the systemic traditionalism of government is closely engrained with paper-based processes, an important vice on the more mobile and collaborative workforce found in the technology sector—and built upon the very devices and processes being created and marketed by these same companies.

Secondly, and externally, despite a widening range of stakeholder engagements and pressures to improve corporate governance, market-driven accountability regimes remain less complex than those of the state. Whereas technology companies are catering to, and working in concert with, a subset of society embracing technological change, governments must remain relevant to not only these individuals but also typically larger segments of their populations more trepid or hostile to online and digital innovation.

Despite such differences, it is notable that the flagship companies leading the digital and mobile revolution have been confronted with a similar and paradoxical set of choices concerning their own internal and governance schemes—namely, tensions between centralization and democratization. Perhaps most telling in this regard is the case of Google and its surprising and seemingly counterintuitive portrayal by Nicolas Carr as a proponent of many of the same bureaucratic principles that have shaped government's evolution, notably specialization and automation.

Carr's assertion is that Google's inherently Taylorian mission for society as a whole is to transform most every decision previously undertaken and reflected upon by humans into an algorithm-inspired calculation:

> More than a hundred years after the invention of the steam engine, the Industrial Revolution had at last found its philosophy and its philosopher. Taylor's tight industrial choreography—his "system," as he liked to call it—was embraced by manufacturers throughout the country and, in time, around the world. Seeking maximum speed, maximum efficiency, and

---

[2] With the exception of Research in Motion, based in Waterloo, Canada, a region known in Canada as Silicon Valley North.

maximum output, factory owners used time-and-motion studies to organize their work and configure the jobs of their workers. The goal, as Taylor defined it…was to identify and adopt, for every job, the "one best method" of work and thereby to effect "the gradual substitution of science for rule of thumb throughout the mechanic arts."

Taylor's system is still very much with us; it remains the ethic of industrial manufacturing. And now, thanks to the growing power that computer engineers and software coders wield over our intellectual lives, Taylor's ethic is beginning to govern the realm of the mind as well. The Internet is a machine designed for the efficient and automated collection, transmission, and manipulation of information, and its legions of programmers are intent on finding the "one best method"—the perfect algorithm—to carry out every mental movement of what we've come to describe as "knowledge work."

Google's headquarters, in Mountain View, California—the Googleplex—is the Internet's high church, and the religion practiced inside its walls is Taylorism. Google, says its chief executive, Eric Schmidt, is "a company that's founded around the science of measurement," and it is striving to "systematize everything" it does. Drawing on the terabytes of behavioral data it collects through its search engine and other sites, it carries out thousands of experiments a day, according to the Harvard Business Review, and it uses the results to refine the algorithms that increasingly control how people find information and extract meaning from it. What Taylor did for the work of the hand, Google is doing for the work of the mind.

The company has declared that its mission is "to organize the world's information and make it universally accessible and useful." It seeks to develop "the perfect search engine," which it defines as something that "understands exactly what you mean and gives you back exactly what you want." In Google's view, information is a kind of commodity, a utilitarian resource that can be mined and processed with industrial efficiency. The more pieces of information we can "access" and the faster we can extract their gist, the more productive we become as thinkers (Carr 2008).

This portrayal, not surprisingly, ignited a firestorm of debate and exchange and led to one major American research body to probe the viewpoints of various experts with regard to Carr's assertions and the actions and societal influences of Google. The case for the company's democratization ethos was perhaps best put forth by a company executive in terms of empowering widening segments of the global populous with access and opportunities previously unattainable:

I would (also) like to say that Carr has it mostly backwards when he says that Google is built on the principles of Taylorism [the institution of time-management and worker-activity standards in industrial settings]. Taylorism shifts responsibility from worker to management, institutes a standard method for each job, and selects workers with skills unique for a specific job. Google does the opposite, shifting responsibility from management to the worker, encouraging creativity in each job, and encouraging workers to shift among many different roles in their career.... Carr is of course right that Google thrives on understanding data. But making sense of data (both for Google internally and for its users) is not like building the same artifact over and over on an assembly line; rather it requires creativity, a mix of broad and deep knowledge, and a host of connections to other people. That is what Google is trying to facilitate." (Peter Norvig, Google Research Director)[3]

---

[3]http://pewresearch.org/pubs/1499/google-does-it-make-us-stupid-experts-stakeholders-mostly-say-no

Does Google contribute to an automation of cognitive processes—thereby reducing freedom and flexibility—or instead unleash wider opportunities for both individual and collective learning and engagement? Is Google a model of machinery (albeit in a new form) or a driver of greater empowerment and mobility?

Such questions implicitly pervade subsequent chapters while underscoring how bureaucracy remains a prevalent theme of the emerging mobility era, not only within government but across all sectors of society. Most any organization—private, public, or nonprofit—faces not a stark choice between bureaucracy and networks but a much more nuanced set of design choices across both realms, with the nature of government accountability rendering the pace of change in this sector often more incremental and contested.

In shifting from machinery to mobility, then, the overriding public sector challenge is not complete abandonment of bureaucracy but instead one of embracing and mobilizing the forces of new governance (outlined in this chapter) into more responsive and adaptive governance systems both administratively and politically. Such is the task at hand and the focus of the next chapter.

Chapter 3
Cognition and Place

Containment Vs. Empowerment

Viewed through a bureaucratic prism, a mobile workforce is unwieldy, uncontrollable, and unproductive. Conversely, the premise of "S.O.C.I.A.L." and like-minded Web 2.0 infused governance models discussed in the preceding chapter is precisely the opposite—namely, that bureaucracy is poorly suited to collaboration and engagement, much as its ethos of control runs counter to today's imperative of empowerment. An environment of heightened mobility and virtualization, consequently, necessitates alterations to the intellectual, physical, and organizational dimensions of organizational activity for public servants working within the confines of government.

Such change and reform are more often than not incremental rather than beginning from anew. As such, even today, it is more accurate to speak of the new and requisite mixes of bureaucratic and more networked forms of organization destined to significantly reshape the public sector workforce and workplace as mobility becomes both a technological and social reality. Yet despite a growing online universe and widening virtualization, the importance of geographic proximity remains a central element of socioeconomic development and public sector organization: such tensions between the traditional patterns of place (and the physicality of both organizational and jurisdictional governance models) and more virtual communications and interactivity are central to the focus of this chapter.

In addition to where people work are equally important matters of how and why they do so. While the broad principles and parameters of post-bureaucratic governance are identifiable—mass collaboration, collective intelligence, and participative engagement—transforming such principles into workable organizational models invariably gives rise to new challenges less apparent or nonexistent in a more traditional government world founded on bureaucratic processes and control. These challenges are intertwined with important changes to both the cognitive capacities of individuals working in government and the physicality of organizing and

J. Roy, *From Machinery to Mobility: Government and Democracy in a Participative Age*, Public Administration and Information Technology 2, DOI 10.1007/978-1-4614-7221-6_3, © Springer Science+Business Media New York 2013

conducting such work. Whereas the traditional machinery of government denotes hierarchical specialization within a strictly defined bureaucratic space, mobility and post-bureaucratic governance face newfound freedoms but also novel risks.

The purpose of this chapter, therefore, is to explore the shifting cognitive and spatial dimensions to public sector organization and how such dimensions reflect and are interrelated with the tensions presented in the previous chapter (between a bureaucratic-centric and control-laden model of machinery and an alternative governance schematic premised upon mobility).

Passion and Peril

The traditional prism of machinery of government implies a limited and precisely defined skill set for public servants, rooted by a deferential cultural of hierarchical authority that, as discussed in the previous chapter, is suited for an environment of scarce and specialized information flows cresting upward toward the apex of organizational leadership. With the exception of the most senior managers (often interacting with elected officials in more nuanced and varied manners), a prototypical public servant's cognitive demands are thus closely aligned, shaped, and constrained by bureaucratic structures and vertical reporting relationships. Freedom of judgment is thereby the exception rather than the norm.

Nonetheless, despite the ongoing bureaucratic traditions in many aspects of public sector activity, few would argue that following orders is the most important trait of a government worker. As a basis for innovative and participative management, for example, one management theorist postulates in rather stark terms the relative contribution of different human capabilities for an organization's ability to create value (Hamel and Breen 2007):

Passion	35 %
Creativity	25 %
Initiative	20 %
Intellect	15 %
Diligence	5 %
Obedience	0 %

Hamel adds that while obedience may serve a purpose in organizational life since there are times when rules must be obeyed, the source of competitive advantage and value added lies elsewhere: "I'm arguing that rule-following employees are worth zip in terms of the competitive advantage they generate…Today, obedience, diligence and expertise can be bought for next to nothing. From Bangalore to Gangzhou, they have become global commodities" (p. 59, ibid.).

Despite this private sector orientation, the implications for government are no less profound—even as the relatively greater importance of rules in government settings can certainly lead to legitimate arguments for a somewhat greater attachment to obedience and diligence. While public sector employees require appreciation for how value creation differs within a context of public interest and democratic accountability, governments also rely increasingly on passion, creativity, and initiative (a point increasingly recognized by governments themselves).

Another critical insight from Hamel is the link between individual creativity and conversation. With innovation shown to be a dynamic and interactive process intertwined with serendipitous discovery, cultivating productive conversations both within and across organizational boundaries is an essential ingredient of collective intelligence (ibid.). The challenge here for government is twofold: firstly to shift away from the traditional public servant mindset of anonymous and deferential behavior and, secondly, to respond to the demographic transformation emerging within the ranks of the public service. Younger generations of knowledge workers—especially the most educated—are the most rapid adapters to the new technologies and communities afforded by Web 2.0, and the manner by which they converse is no less transformative. Accordingly, the spreading of social media is rapidly altering the conversational patterns of public servants and how they become informed and interact (Conabree 2011; Dean and Webb 2011).

This evolving nature of such conversations and how they are both encouraged and leveraged into innovation and action is closely intertwined with the existence of more horizontal and networked forms of trust than have typically characterized a predominantly hierarchical public sector. In other words, conversations are more closely aligned with empowerment than containment. Research in recent years demonstrates that in both the workplace and society at large, trust is increasingly a product of direct forms of engagement with individuals viewed as peers, with a corresponding decline of trust in traditional authoritative structures such as organizational positions and professional credentials (Roy 2006; Carr-West 2009). Lowe underlines the consequence for public sector managers—namely, that a high-trust workplace is high performing because employees are more than engaged—they are passionate about their work and feel inspired to further their organization's goals (Lowe 2006).

As the scope of collaboration expands, so too does demand for workers who can function in an increasingly fluid and complex organizational context. A global survey conducted by the Economist Intelligence Unit, in association with KPMG, is one of many such efforts to articulate the prototype of the future public servant as someone able to navigate complexity both internally and externally. In terms of roles perceived by public sector executives as destined to be most essential in 2020, two areas garnered the most support (62 % and 32 %, respectively) by a wide margin (Economist Intelligence Unit 2006): "Complex knowledge based roles that are primarily outward-facing and require developed communication and judgment skills; and complex knowledge based roles that are primarily inward-looking and require developed communication and inward looking skills" (p. 64). A more recent study on the "future of government" by the World Economic Forum is similar in its conclusions (World Economic Forum 2011).

Information Overload

Despite such currents for passion and creativity, and thus more organizational fluidity, countervailing risks are apparent. In one manner, more flexible organizational models that facilitate collaboration are said to be desirable and even necessary (as discussed in the previous chapter). To be innovative and citizen centric, public servants must thus become adept at various skills and roles to focus on better and often more integrated outcomes. In such an environment, accordingly, multitasking and greater skills and task agility are viewed as an essential attribute of a more fluid set of organizational roles and interrelationships. The cognitive demands on public servants, therefore, rise sharply—much as the capacity to address them is facilitated by a more mobile digital architecture that empowers public servants with information to make better judgment both individually and collaboratively.

Conversely, a widening body of research underscores the perils of multitasking and information overload for both individuals and organizations. The root of the matter for the individual is twofold: first, the ability to focus effectively on any specific task and, second, the freedom to think in a reflective and concentrated manner rather than skimming the surface of an endless deluge of e-mails and web links. On both points, multitasking and interacting within an environment of information abundance and more complex and fluid governance processes carry important costs—costs more likely to escalate in a public sector environment where these new governance processes and mindsets are struggling to coexist with traditional bureaucratic values and structures.

The first issue speaks to an important managerial challenge as governments strive to become post-bureaucratic in an information-intensive environment. As boundaries become more fluid, collaboration can spur greater information sharing that quite often, in turn, translates into an overflowing (digital) inbox. Middle managers pay the highest price here, forced to navigate and filter, upward and downward and laterally, as greater demands for networked decision-making and an abundance of information sources and flows generate distraction, anxiety, and overload (Roman et al. 2010).

The second and closely related issue speaks to the nature and nurturing of creativity and innovation both individually and organizationally. A growing number of studies demonstrate that multitasking alters cognitive behavior in ways that limit and even destabilize individual abilities (Ritchel 2010). We have access to more and more knowledge, but according to some, a more scattered and less methodical mindset results. Carr is one of the most prominent spokespersons for the perils of multitasking and information overload. His 2008 commentary in *The Atlantic* magazine, "Is Google Making Us Stupid," sparked much debate including both vitriolic and thoughtful responses (as noted and discussed in the previous chapter in terms of Carr's bureaucratic portrayal of Google's mission and resulting societal impacts).

His subsequent and related book, *The Shallows: What the Internet Is Doing to Our Brains*, explores the neurological underpinnings of his arguments as well as the wider implications for society ever more informed but with diminished capacities for long-term memory and inward and thoughtful reflection and analysis:

> We don't constrain our mental powers when we store new long-term memories. We strengthen them. With each expansion of our memory comes an enlargement of our intelligence. The Web provides a convenient and compelling supplement to personal memory—but when we start using the Web as a substitute for personal memory, by bypassing the inner processes of consolidation, we risk emptying our minds of their riches. (p. 192, Carr 2010)

Artists have long understood and struggled with such challenges, mixing commerce, connectivity, and creativity in new ways. Often, however, performers are most likely to be regularly tweeting and updating their Facebook page while on tour or promoting a new creation. There can then be lengthy intervals where outward silence reigns, as the creative process demands inward reflection and freedom from distraction. A similarly oriented and equally contested quote from Cain—writing on the quiet but threatened power of introverted skill sets—drives such choices and lifestyle and workspace tailoring—namely, that "solitude is a source of innovation" (Cain 2012). By contrast, however, Lehrer describes how William Shakespeare came to be one of history's great writers through incessant socialization within London's vibrant cultural scene (and even a heavy dose of what would by contemporary standards be considered plagiaristic borrowing from the works of others (Lehrer 2012)).[1]

While public service is not artistry, the analogy is nonetheless important. Any government reform strategy or executive speech today highlights the centrality of innovation and creativity, and so it bears asking if and how these core competencies are nurtured and expanded. Yet there is a real danger within large and traditionally hierarchical organizations that an infrastructure of connectivity may subsume managers in a futile attempt to simply keep up with multiplying informational demands and tasks of nominal value.

Such dangers are hardly new, but their relevance is intensifying. An article in *McKinsey Quarterly* offers guidance on "recovering from information overload" and calls upon senior managers to take heed of warning signs and apply thoughtful, disciplined strategies to ensure appropriate boundaries are in place (Dean and Webb 2011). The alternative is an incessant form of multitasking to simply stay afloat (or more dire consequences in terms of anxiety and stress that can quickly spread throughout the ranks of an organization), with greatly diminished personal and collective capacities for creative and reflective activity. For society more broadly, there is widening evidence of growing anxiety and stress levels due at least in part to the porous nature of constant and distributed work demands (Duxbury and Higgins 2012).

An important caveat here is demographic differentiation across current and aspiring government managers. Mid-career professionals are much more likely to identify with the arguments of Carr and others since they themselves are living

---

[1] Regrettably, the author of this book himself fell victim to the related fraudulent practice of fabricating quotes (specifically quotes attributed to Bob Dylan), a scandal leading to his resignation in July 2012 from various prominent media affiliations. The absence of intellectual property protection during Shakespeare's carries relevance to present tensions between proprietary forms of information and open source, a theme returned to in the subsequent chapter.

through technological changes that provide both flexibility and disruption. Younger people are much more inclined to view Carr as a middle-age Luddite bemoaning change (a charge Carr acknowledges and seeks to dispel). There are real indications that tomorrow's managers shall be ever more seamless in their deployment of technology across increasingly fluid private spaces and workplaces. For today's generations growing up digital—the so-called Generation C first presented above and more likely to be sharing ideas via cloud-based programs than working autonomously on desktop computers, multitasking, and real-time collaboration—much of it online, is simply a way of life and there is no comparator.

While it is important to guard against overgeneralization, since many young people also understand the value and importance of artistic creation (much as they can be prone to the stresses of information and online overload), these new and more diversified realities must be appropriately addressed. The workplace of the future will thus be one that aligns the requisite amount of process, physically and virtually, with a much greater leveraging of mobility, freedom, and collective forms of intelligence driven by a more participative web. For many young public servants today seeking change and reform, the hope is to import the creative and empowered aspect of their personal and civic lives into their careers and into a more flexible and virtual workplace (LeBlanc 2012).

Such attitudes are driven by growing interdependencies across professional and personal pursuits and a transcending of employment and home and community boundaries facilitated by virtualization. As a result, aside from new pressures on cognitive capacities and identities, it is equally important to reconsider the geography of government organization and the new interplay of virtual and physical spaces and places in a public sector world shaped by both traditional machinery connotations of bureaucracy and more fluid and flexible architectures of mobility.

The Enduring (and Evolving) Importance of Proximity

Whereas initial waves of enthusiasm for online life and virtual organizations often pointed to the surmounting of traditional geographic patterns and limitations in favor of new patterns of interacting and organizing, a much more familiar—and indeed paradoxical—set of contours has instead emerged.

There is an important analogy here with the rhetoric of globalization—a process that some suggested would mark the beginning of the end for traditional political structures such as nation-states as well as industrial structures of a more geographically confined and often proximity-driven economy. By contrast, Naisbitt's characterization of a "global–local paradox" much more aptly captured the offsetting tendencies of communities and organizations in all sectors to become both more globalized and more localized (Paquet and Roy 1995; Coe et al. 2001). The rise of the Internet would, in fact, accentuate this depiction—as the term "smart communities" was first coined in order to capture the marrying of virtual and geographic innovation within more creative and connected communities (Eger 2012).

Several decades later, similar patterns are now on display in mixing the physical and virtual realms of social and organizational life. A recent analysis of social media activity, for example, reveals both globalizing and localizing tendencies of social media forums such as Twitter (Takhteyev et al. 2012). The study underscores how in an increasingly mobile and cosmopolitan society it is not unusual to witness new migrants leveraging Facebook and other like-minded sites to communicate and interact with distant friends and relatives while also interacting locally via a range of personal and professional ties that shape the daily choices and routines of residents and communities. Moreover, social media sites such as Foursquare are explicitly premised on finding ways to align virtual and real-time settings into new forms of commercial and civic opportunities, an avenue pursued by all Internet giants as mobile devices such as smartphones and tablets expand location-based information mining and service offerings.

Such parallel trends are both perverse and logical at the same time. They are perverse given the inherent capacity of the Internet to transcend the limits of physicality: witness the rise of virtual corporations and networked social movements across the globe. Yet the logic stems from the largely market-driven paradigm of connectivity pursued by most countries which reinforces the competitive advantages of larger urban dwellings over smaller cities and more rural and remote communities.

In New York's January 2012 State of the State address, for example, the Governor pledged one billion dollars to attract businesses to the languishing City of Buffalo. By contrast, 1 month prior, the City of New York announced it was spending a fraction of this amount, 100 million dollars in a massive partnership with a consortium of universities led by Cornell to develop a new city within a city, an island cluster of science and technology meant to one-day rival California's Silicon Valley as a magnet for students, researchers, entrepreneurs, and investors. That would be *the* Silicon Valley—repeatedly, over the years—declared past its prime due to high costs and congestion and the advent of globalization and low-cost virtual networks. Today, Silicon Valley is home to Apple, Facebook, and Google, to name but the most obvious, remaining the world's enduring laboratory for the powerfully magnetic forces of proximity in underpinning economic innovation and entrepreneurial creativity.

Another industry, the financial services sector, is similarly instructive, viewed as an important reference point for governments looking to better leverage online service channels and improve the user experience by rebalancing physical and virtual operations for a large and demographically and social diverse clientele. With respect to mobility and the evolving patterns of work organization and service delivery, then, the experiences of traditional banks in Canada (having escaped the volatility that has consumed much of this industry globally) are thus a worthwhile deviation from our public sector storyline.

Despite early suggestive hype, the rise of the Internet has not doomed the traditional bricks and mortar structure of the banking industry: the neighborhood branch. Indeed, while some smaller and remote communities have witnessed consolidation (and tensions surrounding access not unlike public sector strategies surrounding government service centers), many urban centers have witnessed a steady expansion of such in-person, street level facilities. The experience of TD Waterhouse—attempting in recent years to gain a foothold via expansion in the US market—is revealing in this regard: a central tenant of their effort, for instance, has been the opening of several new flagship branches in key urban centers such as New York City. In Canada, similarly, the Canadian Bankers Association characterizes the branch as "the personal touch" and still "a vital part of banking in Canada," the primary channel of 18 % of Canadians in a 2012 industry survey vs. 47 % selecting online as their main preference (Canadian Bankers Association 2012).

Across such a fluid multichannel setting, the form and purpose of a physical branch have altered considerably (as reflected in the "personal touch" characterization) from prior generations. Aside from a source of familiarity for many elderly clients, branches today are mainly meeting places and facilities for complex and tailored services as opposed to routinized transactions that have, for the most part, gravitated to telephony and online channels. To accommodate these new service patterns, frontline staff must be trained in accordance with various scenarios and decision trees involving multiple agents and meeting locales (such as meeting rooms allocated less often by person than by task and time intervals). In addition to the core branch facility, a cadre of independent and affiliated specialists (such as mortgage brokers) often roam throughout communities visiting client sites and meeting with individuals in cafes and homes, extending virtual work patterns accordingly. In this regard, within any city or region, a banking enterprise is increasingly networked in form and function.

The banking sector also remains, nonetheless, a highly centralized industry when viewed through a wider geographic prism. Head offices of most all major financial institutions based in and around Toronto's downtown financial corridors intersecting at the corner of Bay and King Streets, respectively. In a manner that resembles provincial and federal governments clustered in their respective capital cities, this concentration of power facilitates intra-industry mobility, formalized alliances and informal networking, and perhaps above all else a sharing of a talent pool that, like programmers and venture capitalists swarming to Silicon Valley, features a strong self-reinforcing dynamic across companies, the educational sector, and supporting institutions.

In short, the clustering of human capital and work patterns within organizational structures is a key attribute of any large sector public or private. For many large industries, notably the technology sector, virtualization and globalization go hand in hand with the localizing tendencies of economic clusters and the "rise of the creative class" within mainly urban confines (Florida 2005). Despite the predominance of centers of finance globally (notably New York, London, and Tokyo), the banking sector shares some geographic attributes of government with respect to national structures and boundaries and a simultaneous emphasis on a national financial capital and a more dispersed presence across cities and communities as with the aforementioned Canadian example. As banks have shifted to an online landscape, the twofold mobility challenge includes surmounting bureaucratic tendencies and constraints within the head office setting while coordinating across a multichannel service architecture that still includes grassroots operations that, in turn, require flexibility and engagement on a microscale.

Tele-Government

For government less globalized and more confined by national processes and boundaries, the agglomeration of private and public infrastructure and the separate and interacting human resource needs of both realms typically accentuates the economic importance of capital cities housing concentrated knowledge workforces within urbanized settings. The most illustrative example of such physical concentration is the American Capital, Washington, DC, home to an estimated 300,000 federal public servants and an additional cadre of consultants and suppliers that together represents one of the country's largest concentrations of knowledge and human capital.[2] Whether such density denotes bureaucratic excess and overcentralization merits reflection and debate, though there can be little question that the region presents a critical laboratory exhibiting the inertia of geographic proximity along with escalating human and ecological costs of housing workers in traditional offices and having them commute in largely traditional patterns to and from home.

The advent of mobile devices such as smartphones and tablets greatly facilitates the widening of distributed and virtual forms of work. A 2012 study of the US federal government by an American research organization, MeriTalk (the Government IT Network), sought to quantify the cost savings and productivity improvements of mobility. Their estimated $2.6 billion in annual productivity gains is based upon an assumption of a 10 % improvement in productivity through the systemic deployment and usage of mobility devices across the federal government. While such a figure is partly aspirational in nature—undoubtedly underplaying retraining, technical, and transitioning costs—it is based upon surveys with federal public servants and their viewpoints regarding potential improvements and savings achievable but unutilized at present. It is also not unimportant that such a direction emerges in a governmental setting with some measure of political support and interest, a prerequisite to addressing the immense organizational complexity and significant resistance at play.

For example, in a symbolic gesture, President Obama signed the Telework Enhancement Act of 2010 (also labeling himself as the nation's "Teleworker" in Chief) mandating all federal departments and agencies to develop and implement formal teleworking strategies. Such an impetus has yielded some early yet encouraging findings with respect to the promotion and usage of teleworking arrangements across the American federal government. In its 2012 report to Congress on this topic, the US Office of Personnel Management articulates the evolution of teleworking from an individual benefit to a more strategic basis of organizational and societal value:

> Aligned with agency strategy and mission, telework supports achievement of objectives increasingly important for operation of an efficient and effective Federal Government, including cost savings and improved performance, and maximizing organizational productivity.

---

[2] Underpinned by various metrics such as educational degrees and related indices of the knowledge workforce, many DC-area proponents characterize the region as the country's second leading home of technology workers after Silicon Valley in California.

Developed as a strategic program, telework is a powerful agency recruitment and retention tool with the capacity to improve the competitive position of the Federal Government for recruiting and retaining the best possible workforce.

Leveraged as a management tool, telework mitigates potential disruptions to workplace productivity (e.g., severe weather). (p. 6, United States Office of Personnel Management 2012)

Despite modest progress in the proportion of federal government employees engaged in teleworking arrangements (just over one-quarter of all full-time employees deemed eligible), survey findings of those working at least part of their week from a remote location—most typically their home—underscore the individualized benefits accruing to such workers:

In comparison to non-teleworkers facing barriers to telework, teleworkers are more likely to report knowing what is expected of them on the job and feeling as though they are held accountable for results. Teleworkers also reported a greater sense of empowerment, higher job satisfaction, and a greater desire to stay at their current job. (p. 9, ibid.)

With respect to tensions between machinery and mobility, there are three important implications stemming from such findings for governments. Firstly, the advent of mobility as both technological infrastructure and societal mindset greatly accentuates both the feasibility of alternative work arrangements for widening portions of the workforce. Secondly, the strategic and wider societal benefits from more flexible and virtual work patterns are similarly much more attainable should efforts be put in place to achieve them. Thirdly, resistance to such directions is often widespread, engrained by the traditions of bureaucratic organization and conduct.

In Canada, the 2012 federal budget reflected much duality—with a signature restructuring and significant cutback of the public service most prominently felt in the national capital city (Ottawa), on the one hand, and a simultaneous pledge to examine ways to reduce federal travel costs of public servants through the utilization of virtual venues such as "tele-presence" (explicitly noted in p. 228 of the 2012 federal budget speech as one means of doing so). Similarly, the Provincial Government of Nova Scotia announced its intention in the spring of 2012 to decentralize dozens of core positions across three major provincial departments from Halifax to different communities across the province and immediately faced controversy as most affected public servants refused relocation (CBC News 2012).

These sorts of examples illustrate the complexity of government reform in the mobile era as a set of political and organizational factors shaping community development locally and public sector performance within local jurisdictions as well as for a country as a whole. What remains less clear and often contested is whether initiatives such as teleworking policies and virtual conferencing represent little more than peripheral experimentations or instead the beginnings of a truly more novel and strategic approach to public sector organization in a networked and mobility-driven environment. The Canadian examples are indicative of the former and a more trepid path for change, whereas the current American experience suggests that the latter perspective may well be gaining some traction—in keeping with mobile realities socially and organizationally on the one hand and an important political impetus on the other hand. Yet, as noted, resistance runs deep. A mobility mindset and corresponding innovation in governance thus necessitate a more meaningful reframing of the both the conduct and place of work.

"Work Is What You Do—Not a Place You Go"

This subtitle is a quote from a 2008 UK report entitled Working Beyond Walls, which examines the government workplace of the future in a thoughtful, multidimensional, and holistic manner (Hardy et al. 2008). The report presents five levels of escalating organizational commitment to alternative work arrangements and like-minded flexibility in governance: ad hoc, experimental, selectively deployed, formalized, and institutionalized (ibid.).

Whereas the preceding examples of telework within the US federal government may reflect level two or level three examples (of experimentation and selective deployment), achieving something akin to level five requires more ambition and deepened reform both structurally and culturally. A central step in this regard is the decoupling of managerial processes from the spatial and cognitive confines of a traditional office in favor of alternative and more varied schemes more accommodating of choice and diversity in terms of lifestyles and skill sets:

> Work and the people who do it are increasingly found beyond the boundaries of the office and therefore beyond reach of traditional command-and-control management. This throws down new challenges on the significance of design. The future for an increasing proportion of the government workforce will lie beyond physical boundaries, in highly connected, geographically spread locations.

> As office work frees itself from the confines of single building boundaries to become distributed across locations and time, then design outcomes begin to matter in different ways. If the organizational office is to have a role in the new world of work, it has to attract and retain people, and to do that it must compete with a wide range of other physical—as well as virtual—work options. (p. 15, ibid.)

Within bureaucratic settings, physically defined structures such as the office cubicle and the desk denote and constrain worker status and action. The initial layers of telecommunications infrastructure—namely, the landline telephone and desktop computer—merely accentuated the importance of such physical concentration, most especially in large organizations that had already developed work processes around hierarchical specialization and routine patterns of conduct.

In a mobile world, conversely, an alternative conceptualization of the workplace is needed in order to begin to facilitate the orchestration of more flexible and adaptive governance models that both empower and enable individuals to blend physical and virtual venues and tools in tailored and often self-determined manners:

> The effect of all this connectivity is that people can work anywhere at any time, including the office, the home and a range of other 'third place' work-settings…Designing the office of the future will require acknowledgment of its role as a place for fostering organizational solidarity and for it to signify and express the values and beliefs of the organization. As a consequence there will be a development towards the creation of office interiors that are more richly layered with physical and electronic information, telling stories or conveying messages about the organization and its work. (p. 25, ibid.)

From a generational perspective, the realization of more flexible and agile models of work may well face barriers of resistance stemming from the incremental pace of change associated with cadres of office workers who have spent years—and in many cases decades, conducting tasks and interacting with peers within traditional office confines. Moreover, the sorts of dangers stemming from constant connectivity and information overload must also be accounted for not only with respect to demographic evolutions (and the necessity of embracing greater virtualization) but also in terms of the appropriate blending of physical and virtual workspaces in manners that facilitate creativity and collaboration in accordance with performance objectives and measurable outcomes.

With government's traditional top-down mentality emphasizing containment and control, there is a significant risk of languishing behind private sector organizations, thereby accentuating recruitment and retention pressures and limiting the emergence of experimentation and flexibility (Macmillan et al. 2008; Serrat 2010). As information flows accelerate and multitasking demands and potentials augment, uniformity of work styles becomes a counterproductive notion. Instead, as traditional geographic and spatial confines become increasingly challenged and loosened, a multipronged approach is necessary in orchestrating integrative change for both the governance of public sector entities and the wider societal implications of virtualization.

Aligning closely with the US federal government's articulation of teleworking benefits for workers, agencies, and society as a whole, three similarly core dimensions are offered by a UK consultancy specializing in "smarter work practices":

- Measurable business benefits—improved service delivery, increased productivity, reduced costs, reduced absence, improved staff retention, greater organisational agility
- Improved environmental performance—travel reduction, reduced resource consumption, better environmental performance of (fewer) buildings
- Improved social performance—better work-life balance for staff, greater choice, autonomy and motivation, improved staff satisfaction, widening the recruitment pool for staff and increasing diversity. (p. 34, Lake 2011)

These three levels are pertinent to the sorts of teleworking benefits found within the US federal government reviewed earlier on—as well as the need for a wider prism of formalized and institutionalized change predicated upon these sorts of multifaceted benefit streams. For example, in the US health-care sector, from 2007 to 2010, one large private insurance company, SCAN Health, undertook a distributed work program that would yield the following benefits: a 40 % return on investment for program development and deployment, 38 % reduction in cost of workplace support, 18 % increase in productivity, a reduction in provisioning (i.e., processing of claims and payments) time from 12 weeks to 3 days, and a decrease in travel to work by 20 % for program employees (Ware and Grantham 2010).

Openness and Engagement

As mobility spreads as both a virtual infrastructure and a social mindset—resonating particularly with younger generations of managers entering the workforce—the effective embracement and deployment of new governance capacities become paramount to traditional human resource challenges such as recruitment and retention, as well as a wider and more strategic prism of employee trust and organizational performance.

Already, recruiting via social media has become an increasingly common practice across both industry and government: LinkedIn has over 85 million members from more than 200 member countries, for example, and monster.com claims to house more than 150 million resumes. In responding to this new demographic and their altering values and behavioral patterns, what matters more than an online presence on social media sites is the online and continual conduct of organizations in such virtualized spaces. The agency established by the Provincial Government of Ontario (Canada) to recruit health-care workers emphatically underscores that social media recruiting is not about broadcasting but rather about conversing:

> Participate in the conversation. Respond to people regardless of whether they write positively or negatively about your community/organization. Talk with them about their experiences and help to resolve issues, whether or not those are related to physician recruitment. Every time you engage with others, you help to build relationships and the image of your community or organization. (p. 15, HealthForceOntario 2011)

Driven by such trends, the Obama impetus described above, and the advent of Web 2.0 tools and mindsets, the impacts of mobility on both the workforce and workplace are rapidly evolving in manners increasingly recognized and embraced by the public sector as well. As the US Department of Defense (itself a notable example of what many regard as emblematic of traditional bureaucratic authority and culture) articulates:

> The transformation of the workplace is just beginning…The workplace of the future will be radically different from today's preconceived workplace that involves hard-wired equipment, multiple cubicles, and 9 to 5 workdays. The future promises more flexibility, more mobility, and more independence, while at the same time, helping employers to get the most out of every employee. Web 2.0 tools are already helping to create a seamless work environment where employees can easily transition from one task to another without having to move from one tool to another. Additionally, they will create a level of transparency that affords employees an opportunity to view the work of others and makes employees more accountable.[3]

As acknowledged and explained both in this chapter and its predecessor, any evolution from a predominantly physical environment to one more virtual is bound to be contested due to the gravitational pull of bureaucratic underpinnings that equate organizational process and risk mitigation with and location-specific monitoring and control. While such a mindset may well prove unsustainable due to demographic and technological forces tied to the advent of mobility, realizing the institutionalization of more distributed work patterns nonetheless requires major systemic change from current governance models and practices both

---

[3] Extracted from an online commentary on "Shaping the Workplace Through Web 2.0 Technologies," CIO Office of the US Department of Defense. *Source*: http://dodcio.defense.gov/Home/Initiatives/NetGenerationGuide/ShapingtheWorkplaceThroughWeb20Technologies.aspx

administratively and politically. The main contours of such changes are examined going forward.

Beginning with the next chapter, the first theme requiring careful examination is the evolution of today's digital and increasingly mobile-laden technological infrastructure and the emergence of the cloud as a more participative governance model far less rooted in traditional and intertwined notions of proprietary property and place. Many of the environmental and social performance benefits noted above are, in a very real sense, built upon the foundations of cloud-enabled platforms that, if leveraged well, can facilitate the more collaborative and distributed work models discussed above.

Much as bureaucracy denotes a powerful inert anchor against such reforms organizationally, similarly powerful traditions of proprietary ownership and information control also characterize this struggle technologically. The next chapter, therefore, examines the central and interrelated topics of openness and ownership as a critical component of public sector adaptation from its bureaucratic foundations—otherwise known as the machinery of government, toward a more networked and participative paradigm aligned with the advent of mobility.

Chapter 4
Openness and Ownership

Transparency and Trust

Yet another paradox of digital life presents itself. Despite the steady expansion of the Internet globally and corresponding promises of e-government to usher in a new era of public sector transparency and heightened accountability, there are widening signs of public distrust instead. The 2009 Global Corruption Barometer produced by Transparency International, for example, reports that nearly one third of those surveyed globally viewed political parties as the most corrupt body in their country, followed by one quarter pointing to public officials and civil servants. Such findings are indicative of a weakened culture of democratic engagement and a growing divide between elected officials and the citizenry (Nabatchi 2010; Roy 2011).

In recent years, the combination of online government and massive stimulus spending by public sector authorities has presented both an opportunity and challenge—in seeking to expedite approvals and investments while also ensure openness and accountability. The first Obama Administration's inaugural and aggressive usage of online reporting in the United States is one such example. The effort features the establishment of an arm's length Recovery Board[1] created to provide oversight and openness; the Board was explicitly mandated to design and maintain an interactive, online portal, enabling citizens, companies, the media, researchers, and special interests to track spending efforts and results. The 2009 "Common Cause Stimulus Transparency, Accountability, and Clean Administration," project aims to

> Promote a model for transparency, accountability, and clean administration of stimulus spending for all levels of government across the country, and develop state and local coalitions made up of diverse stakeholders to insist on full transparency of stimulus spending. Working together, environmental, labour, education, health care and other interest groups will be able to 'drill down' to assess spending in their respective areas and press policymakers and government administrators to use the stimulus money effectively.[2]

---

[1] See http://www.recovery.gov

[2] See http://www.commoncause.org

J. Roy, *From Machinery to Mobility: Government and Democracy in a Participative Age*, Public Administration and Information Technology 2, DOI 10.1007/978-1-4614-7221-6_4, © Springer Science+Business Media New York 2013

Much of this "drilling down" occurs online—and importantly, not simply by lawmakers in Congress but rather by both newly mobilized virtual activists and organized interest groups leveraging this data into wider oversight and policy debates. A similar effort led by civil society organizations in Europe has resulted in openness and transparency in terms of European farm subsidies, a previously secretive data set of recipients and amounts.[3] In both the US and European examples, it is not merely the existence of such websites as repositories of online data that matters—but the potential for wider scrutiny and usage across political, media, industry, and civil society formations.

Conversely, the risk of this sort of online reporting is that while openness increases, such transparency may come at the expense of trust if citizens are merely enabled to view practices and expenditures they deem dubious or ill advised (or alternatively if third party groups falsify or portray governmental action and information for their own subjective purposes). The Obama Administration's efforts highlight the contradictory forces at play. On the one hand, the President's first legislative act in 2009 was an openness directive (the Presidential Memorandum on Transparency and Open Government, underpinning the aforementioned recovery. gov effort as one derivative that followed). Yet despite such movement toward wider transparency, there are many offsetting arguments for the pervasiveness of secrecy throughout the first Obama mandate (Greenwald 2012).

A similar evolution is identifiable in the Canadian Parliamentary model in terms of Prime Minister Harper's 2006 campaign premised on principles of openness and accountability (leading to the passage of the Accountability Act which sought greater limitations and oversight on lobbying and additional Parliamentary scrutiny of budgeting by an independent officer among other reforms). Yet in the years to follow, numerous independent and media voices accused the government of augmenting secrecy, culminating in the 2012 federal budget (the first as a majority government) that comprised a large omnibus bill with a wide cadre of legislative actions only loosely tied together as budget matters and thus passed with little consultation or debate (beyond the overall discussion of the budget globally).[4]

While in all democracies a relatively uncontested notion is to first provide basic budgetary information to citizens on the resources and expenditures of the state—in order to ensure a minimum level of fiscal literacy and public accountability—many argue that facilitated by the Internet and the advent of mobility, much more can and should be done. In this age of greater connectedness and openness and especially in light of the growing potential of Web 2.0 platforms and tools to enable connectivity and conversation, openness and transparency are increasingly coupled with engagement. As the United Nations stated several years ago:

---

[3] See http://www.farmsubsidy.org

[4] On June 4, 2012, more than 500 nonprofit organizations protested government secrecy and passage of the federal omnibus budget legislation by blacking out their own websites for a portion of the day.

For the accountability processes in development management, the engagement of all stake-holders – including civil society organizations, non-governmental organizations, media and the private sector – is crucial. In particular, there has been an increasing emphasis on the need to increase and intensify the involvement of citizens in the decision-making processes, not only in government policy formulation but also in budgeting, public expenditure management and auditing. (p. 48, United Nations Economic and Social Council 2007)

The problem confronted in moving down such a path lies in the incremental imposition of transparency measures—based upon a loose association of the Internet with openness (an association invited and reinforced by governments themselves), upon primarily bureaucratic institutional systems predicated on information scarcity and control (for reasons discussed in Chap. 2). This schism drives the complexity of the relationship between transparency and trust that, in turn, is central to the friction between machinery and mobility.

The consequence leads some groups to call for a deeper rethinking of democratic governance as a direct result of the changing nature of digital technologies and their capacities to foster more genuine and organic forms of transparency. Consider the following two quotes from a testimony to a 2011 UK Parliamentary Committee examining that county's public sector struggles with digital adaptation, the first from a research body (Institute of Creative Technologies) and the second by an open-source software company (Sirius):

(Governments should) move beyond the 'transformational government' programme, which aimed to impose command and control through large centralised databases, towards principles of transparency, openness, and co-operation in which the individual citizen has far more engagement with and control over data and personal information.

Open technologies empower individuals and shift power away from the centre. Open technologies build social cohesion and are socially transformative. Government should be as technologically smart as possible, in the service of productive efficiency and participatory democracy. (p. 9, Public Administration Committee, British House of Commons 2011)

This latter statement's invocation of participatory democracy is central. The aforementioned examples from the American Presidential and Canadian Parliamentary models share foundational principles and structures of representational democracy. Any shift from representational to participative democracy is a highly contested and complex endeavor encompassing multiple viewpoints over both principles and design (an endeavor explored more fully in latter chapters of this book).

As examined in the next section, however, the interplay between evolving societies in the still-nascent mobility era and their democratic systems is at the very least in flux, with contemporary forces for transparency and participation rooted in wider shifts in behavior and values being driven by the spreading of digital infrastructure. Moreover, it is not merely the existence of this infrastructure—but how it is assembled and shared in an environment increasingly characterized by technological contestation between proprietary ownership of information and intellectual property and open-sourced platforms where secrecy and control are shunned and viewed as exceptions rather than norms.

Information, Ideas, and Infrastructure

At the heart of the fluid nexus between openness and ownership that is central to the widening canvas of mobility, we address three specific aspects of public sector adaptation. They include (1) information, (2) ideas, and (3) infrastructure. It is worthwhile exploring the origins and wider implications of each in turn.

Information

As reviewed in the second chapter, the bureaucratic foundations of government—especially the Westminster Parliamentary model—were crafted for an environment of scarce and specialized information, information that politicians and officials in the executive branch seek to contain and shape to their purpose and advantage. In terms of usage and outputs in the realms of services and policies, the corollary here is a communication mindset of taking decisions, crafting a message, and conveying it in polished and edited (and thus often proprietary) form to appropriate constituencies.

Prior to the advent of the Internet, however, democratic governments had themselves recognized the importance of enabling some degree of public openness for purposes of scrutiny, debate, and accountability—pressured as they were by the media, opposition parties, and a gradually more educated and scrutinizing citizenry. The resulting creation of access to information apparatuses in most all democracies thus reflected an attempt to temper the traditionally secretive nature of government with a level of openness nonetheless determined by governments—and in keeping with their own determinations of the appropriate limitations of disclosure and transparency.

Today there are two fundamental problems plaguing these sorts of information management policies and mechanisms.

First, digital technologies have not only mobilized actors from outside of government to demand more information but also encouraged efforts from within the public sector to more formally and regularly scrutinize and filter such requests and responses. Accordingly, governments have increasingly hunkered down in attempts to ensure consistency in disclosing and messaging information or alternatively justifying blockages of access on a widening cadre of policy and political grounds (Roberts 2006). The result is often a poisoning of relations between traditional media intermediaries and governmental authorities, creating a more adversarial dynamic between such parties than has often and typically been the case historically. Access to information system has thus become increasingly formalized and costly processes of reviewing and administering requests—clearly reflecting a mindset of imposed rather than embraced and regularized openness (ibid.).

Secondly, the numerous security provisions of legislation governing information access—bolstered considerably in the aftermath of the September 2001 terrorist attacks—reinforce the preceding points by augmenting the ability of government to withhold information and justify secrecy (Roy 2006, 2012c; Greenwald 2012). The resulting dynamic is often legalistic and increasingly costly to sustain—especially in the face of the mobilization of new online actors promoting openness and disclosure at almost any cost (Owens 2010). While WikiLeaks has been the most prominent example of such a trend, it denotes a wider movement of online access and social media that greatly enhances the ability of both internal whistle-blowers and external activists to seek and share information deemed confidential or otherwise sheltered by public sector authorities. Government, in turn, feels compelled to defend their limitations and boundaries and prosecute those in violation.

In parallel to and to some degree amplifying these problems, the emergence of online government has resulted in highly visible and strategic and political commitments to Internet access and an online ethos of openness in many aspects of governmental operations encompassing both service delivery and policy consultation and development. As we examine further below, governments have even begun to go so far as espousing "open data" strategies that seek to transfer control and usage of vast amounts of previously withheld and internally processed governmental data into the public sphere—in raw form and with unlimited access.

The resulting duality is a contradictory set of actions and approaches oscillating between espousing the benefits of openness and clinging to the necessity of limited disclosure and secrecy. As we have seen, such tensions owe much to the duality between bureaucratic traditions within government and widening demands for alternative governance schemes, but they also are closely intertwined with the evolution of technology and the alteration of ownership over the ideas and infrastructure that underpin digitization and mobility.

Ideas

A world of heightened mobility and new forms of more open and collaborative governance emphasizing and seeking to leverage collective intelligence is one where innovation increasingly becomes an open and collective pursuit. The foundations for such approaches are technological and social.

The rise of open-source software—initially as a direct challenge to not only the market dominance but also the proprietary control and perceived secrecy of Microsoft (often viewed through a bureaucratic-minded prism of control by open-source activists in the software sector)—is illustrative. In an open-sourced environment, individual and corporate notions of ownership of ideas are supplanted by the collective interest and the avoidance or suppression of traditional protection and enforcement mechanisms such as intellectual property patents. Such an evolution and pressures on traditional ownership and their strict assignation of ideas are thus analogous to the challenges examined above—namely, governmental apparatuses designed to manage their "own" information holdings.

Although even today the technology sector remains highly divided between proprietary actors and incentives and more open-sourced alternatives, a much wider acceptance of innovation as an open and shared set of processes is now at the very least engrained in the discourse on digital reforms. The spreading of Web 2.0

experimentation within government is specifically meant to foster collaboration and democratize the creation and exchange of ideas:

> The role of citizens in an open government environment – enriched by open government data – can be one of democratic innovators. In an ongoing open innovation process, citizens can draw on open data, and propose both policy-areas to tackle and technical approaches to take. (p. 186, Maier-Rabler and Huber 2011)

The recasting of governance in terms of expectations and roles is profound. Rather than gathering information and ideas from constituents externally and employees internally via highly regimented and contained mechanisms (shaped by a proprietary mindset), this alternative presentation of openness and ideas begins from the premise that the ownership of information and ideas is fundamentally diffused and shared in ways that cannot be appropriately captured by traditional models of control and accountability (both organizationally and politically).

Yet such directions exemplify the clash between traditional government machinery (where ownership is assigned and protected) and a mindset of mobility that accentuates much more fluid notions of information flows and the generation of ideas. One early study of the usage and acceptance of new social media within the public sector found, for instance, that such tensions are deeply engrained within Canadian Government where ownership remains shaped largely by traditional notions of containment and control. Based upon their own consultations with public servants from across the Canadian public sectors, the authors conclude that

> The most significant impediment to government use of social media is the "clay layer" in management and the hierarchical public service culture.

> Government has not adapted to the promise of new media to liberate information, foster collaboration and openness and promote organizational change. (p. 3, Fyfe and Crookall 2010)

Outside of government, by contrast, the open-source technology community has helped drive—and itself found close alignment with—a philosophical view of the Internet as a platform for freedom and democratization that has, in turn, shaped societal behavior in recent years. Specifically, the explosion of the Internet as a platform for freedom of information and ideas has translated into widespread rejection or circumvention of traditional intellectual property mechanisms—most notably in the music recording (where it bears noting that Apple's success in this industry owes much to the unique marrying of a proprietary product system – iTunes and the iPod, with the rise of online downloading and file sharing) and motion picture sectors (where traditional producers have sought to more forcefully bolster copyright protections, at least against the most egregious examples of illegal downloading and file sharing).

The point here is not to equate open-source development with illegal behavior (although many legal battles stem from their uneasy coexistence—including most notably global patent disputes between Apple and Android-infused Samsung[5]), but

---

[5]This issue was initially flagged in the book's preface, and a related column by this book's author published in late 2012 further illuminates this example: http://www.canadiangovernmentexecutive.ca/article/?nav_id=1056

rather to illustrate the widening ethos of openness that challenges traditional notions of information control and usage and the generation and ownership of ideas. The consequence of this confluence of forces is a mainstream acceptance of cloud computing as a model of software and infrastructure provisioning for the public sector (and indeed all sectors) based much less on traditional corporate ownership and much more on open-sourced operating systems and a correspondingly greater reliance on models of shared and collaborative innovation and participative governance.

Infrastructure

If Microsoft serves as the poster child for the previous era of proprietary software dominance in the corporate and governmental realms, over the last decade Google has come to personify an ethos of openness that transcends and enjoins the three facets of information, ideas, and infrastructure.

Despite human and cognitive challenges in dealing with massive increases in information availability and usage discussed in the preceding chapter, there is no disputing Google's central importance as a facilitator of information via its central mechanism for doing so—namely, the search engine. In this vein, the corporate leviathan has sought to challenge many state efforts (including most notably those of China) to filter and block online content.

The search engine—coupled with a widening array of Web 2.0 tools and platforms to identify, create, and share content online—serves as powerful forces in the aforementioned emergence of open and collective innovation (and in some cases the subversion and rejection of traditional legalistic protections for proprietary content). Yet within this societal transformation, Google has also emerged as a powerful proponent of openness at the nexus of ideas and infrastructure through its development and promotion of freely available tools (such as Gmail and Google Maps to name but two) and the primarily open-sourced, Android operating system underpinning the largest and growing segments of non-Apple mobile devices. In short, despite its own highly proprietary practices pertaining to its search engine algorithms, Google has emerged as a champion of openness and democratization that – along with social media companies (notably Facebook) and cloud-based companies, is devising essentially shared and open platforms for a widening range of software and hardware products.

An early example of the consequences for government came from the City of Nanaimo, British Columbia, on the west coast of Canada which effectively abandoned its prior model of internalized and proprietary and infrastructure and information holdings within the realm of GIS spatial mapping. Citing the benefits of open innovation through greater usage and access and heightened redundancy and security, the municipal government opted for open-source tools (including freely available Google Earth online) and shifted its data imaging that it previously regarded as a proprietary asset to Google's cloud-enabled platform (Birch 2008). Like-minded examples of universities and municipalities embracing cloud-based e-mail systems as alternatives to previously proprietary models were invoked in the introduction of this book, and today most all governments are rethinking their internal IT infrastructure and external outsourcing relationships in accordance with such trends (Wyld 2007, 2010a, b).

Such efforts have not been without controversy and difficulty—as exemplified by the first high-profile encompassing effort by a large American municipal government, the City of Los Angeles, to embrace an administrative infrastructure (including e-mail, data storage, information processing, and enterprise resource planning) provided by Google and its open-source partners. In one notable example, citing security and privacy concerns, the Police Department refused to participate in the venture which has nonetheless persisted in the face of the sorts of early growing pains not unfamiliar to previous era of public–private interactions.

The point, therefore, is not to endorse Google as a desirable or inevitable alternative to traditional proprietary vendors but rather to underscore the duality of both such worlds in the public sector today—and the reasons to believe that in a world of heightened mobility and virtualization, open-sourced and cloud solutions can reasonably be expected to continue their ascent, a claim underpinned by many observers of the technology sector (ibid.).

Such an expectation is already reinforced by the mainstream embracement of the cloud concept by the two predominant proprietary corporations in the technology world today: Apple and Microsoft. Beyond the television ads noted in this book's introduction, Microsoft thus saw fit to create a YouTube video targeted to a public sector audience that trumpets the "power of choice" between cloud-based and proprietary productions and solutions.[6]

The resulting design tensions for government are complex across agency-specific and government-wide dimensions. Traditional dichotomies between insourced and outsourced solutions are thus enjoined by additional variables—customized proprietary models versus open-source variants and if and how to align such options across previously separate organizational silos and electronic systems. Illustratively, we consider, at some length, the reflections of a leading technology and organizational consultancy (Gartner Consulting) describing how such pressures and choices impact the governance of the South African public sector:

> I had a conversation with a client here in South Africa about the large IFMS (Integrated Financial Management System) initiative, which aims to integrate and migrate government finance, HR, asset management, logistics and other line of business solutions, into a single distributed transversal system. Vendors have been selected for two modules, and the State Information Technology Agency is responsible for integration and custom-developed modules. This is a remarkably ambitious project that will ultimately provide a single system to federal as well as provincial departments: I am not aware of anything of comparable scale addressing two tiers of government.

> As far as I understand, departments are somewhat mandated to use this system, so apparently there is no opt-out possible. On the other hand, integration and full deployment are going to take almost a decade: over such a long period of time, it is not unlikely that emerging

---

[6] Source: http://www.youtube.com/watch?v=Rwi5vzjPA_A

cloud-based alternatives become attractive to provinces or federal departments that need to replace their legacy systems but are still waiting for IFMS to be available. Therefore, even where there is no opt-out, centralized solutions will be challenged by lower-cost, more-flexible alternatives over time.

It is even more so in cases where departments and agencies join on a voluntary basis. I wonder whether the 'storefront approach taken by the US GSA (Government Services Agency) (and being considered in the UK too) is a better way to go, assuming that the best role of a central government agency is to become a broker for emerging cloud-based offerings. This is not free from challenges though, such as the definition and enforcement of enterprise standards and vendor selection criteria that allow such a storefront to evolve its offering over time, while maintaining consistency across different solutions.

… How much does the legacy, government-owned infrastructure as well as the contracts around it make the transition to a "private cloud infrastructure" possible, desirable or just financially viable? How far have virtualization programs gone to support all the attributes of cloud computing? How many agencies, and for which workloads, do really need the elasticity, flexibility, fine-grain metering and the other cloud computing attributes? To what extent the governance of a private cloud infrastructure involving several agencies (community cloud in the NIST definition) is effective enough to make sure it does not fall into the same problems that many pre-cloud shared service initiatives ran into? (p. 1, di Maio 2009)

Such context and questions represent an often vexing set of challenges for government managers and political leaders seeking navigation and guidance in this new environment. The main benefits sought by cloud computing enthusiasts are typically the intertwined issues of flexibility and scalability on the one hand and efficiency and innovation on the other hand. The Australian Government, for example, presents these benefits as a set of three key drivers for cloud computing adoption for the public sector: value for money, flexibility, and operational reliability and robustness.[7] Many proponents also add environmental gains as a key consideration, interwoven with flexibility due to the more energy-efficient processing models of large-scale, cloud facilities (providing computing power on demand) in contrast to constantly running computers and servers (Wyld 2010a, b).

For any large organization, the emergence of a utility-like model of cloud computing can mean paying for what you use when you use it (as opposed to building or purchasing entire systems, be they large-scale databases or desktop computers, that rarely if ever run at their full capacity levels). Herein lies how flexibility and scalability can generate efficiency savings, and it is thus no surprise that in the current context of economic uncertainty, cloud computing strategies are often framed first and foremost in terms of cost savings. In the UK, for instance, where the

---

[7]The Australian Government's strategic paper on cloud computing released in 2011 further presents a number of anticipated outcomes for each of these drivers (summarized on page 21). Details of the report (no longer available online in 2012 directly from the government site), and the subsequent steps stemming from it are available online: http://agimo.gov.au/2011/01/07/consultation-draft-australian-government-cloud-computing-strategy-paper/ As of the end of 2012, a version of thereportremainedonlineathttp://agimo.gov.au/2011/01/07/consultation-draft-australian-government-cloud-computing-strategy-paper/

Coalition Government has been aggressively cutting public sector spending to reduce the deficit, cloud solutions have been embraced as one means for doing so:

> The "G-Cloud" strategy came with claims that it could save government £3.2bn of its annual £16bn IT budget – perfectly meeting the chancellor's 20% savings target. The proposal is to replace the current ad-hoc network of department- hosted systems with a dozen dedicated government secure data centres, costing £250m each.

> The G-Cloud plans could support everything from pooled government data centres to a communal email solution, collaboration tools and staff-editable wikis (like Wikipedia, but private). Part of the plan points to the potential of an internal government "app store" so that recommended tools could be shared and distributed among government departments. By 2015, the strategy says, as much as 80% of the government departments could be using this system. (p. 1, Kiss 2010)

The key, initial target of the UK plan is government data centers—and more specifically their consolidation from an estimated 3,500 such centers presently across government (essentially non-cloud systems since they were created in a pre-Internet era) into a small number of perhaps a dozen or so massive data farms to be housed in the UK and operated by cloud providers selected by government. As such, this type of "g-cloud" is in fact indicative of a "private cloud" in so far as it is managed for the exclusive usage of public sector entities (although some elements of a public cloud, more openly accessible to all sectors, may coexist as well if there are areas where security provisions are lessened due to the types of data and services at play). Unlike prior eras of stark choices between insourced and outsourced capacities, an enticing aspect of cloud-based infrastructure is the expansion of access to a wider community of competencies and providers (interlinked via the more shared and distributed governance of cloud systems than traditional proprietary offerings).

Much like organizations such as Apple have sought to align proprietary platforms of operating systems and products with at least partially open communities of application developers (the degree of openness, an important distinguishing feature between Apple and Android operating systems[8]), governments have begun to explore similar participative dynamics via open data initiatives that encourage the free and widespread sharing of public data sets and the creation of tools to make use of such data in a more open environment (consistent with the advent of social media). This sort of openness can enhance the potential for innovation via wider opportunities for flexibility and collaboration within and across organizational boundaries.

It is once again the emphasis on openness and collaboration that justify such expectations and objectives in a cloud environment—enabling individual

---

[8] Apple more directly controls app development for its proprietary platforms and products, whereas Android's operating system is built upon open-source software code and its availability to a wider range of companies and products has facilitated its global expansion at the expense of Apple in many market segments. While RIM has suffered the most at the expense of both systems, the company's early 2013 release of a new operating system (i.e., expected enable for the first time usage of their secure communication exchange service on Apple and Android devices) is illustrative of market pressures for fostering interoperability across such competing platforms: it signifies that RIM can no longer survive as separately walled operating system.

entrepreneurs and large companies alike to partake in a more interoperable online environment where infrastructure is shared and widely accessible. Thus, decisions that governments make in terms embracing private or public clouds carry internal ramifications in terms of public sector organization but also external ones as well in terms of market and community development.

Consistent with and driving government's exploration and gradual adoption of the cloud is a society increasingly mobilized and active with respect to the interplay of information, ideas, and infrastructure—and itself increasingly embracing the cloud. Accordingly, shared ownership and open innovation apply not only to government's own infrastructure but also with respect to its data holdings and interactions with an online citizenry viewed as a potential source of ideas and solutions in a crowd-sourced, cloud-enabled, and mobility-driven environment.

Open Data and "Apps for Democracy"

The emergence of so-called open data initiatives is an extension of this fluidity of ownership that draws elements from across the interrelated realms of information, ideas, and infrastructure. Driven by the rise of social media and collective intelligence on the one hand and the emphasis in recent years on citizen engagement and participatory democracy on the other hand, such strategies are, at their core, about reframing information as a holding and asset of public sector authorities to a shared asset enabling not only oversight and accountability by elected officials but more direct public engagement in the design and delivery of services and solutions.

With respect to the closely related emphasis on "apps," there is a more direct technological association with the phenomena of open communities of application developers devising mini-programs of all sorts to run on various smartphone (and now tablet) devices. The most prominent of such platforms is the Apple operating system and corresponding app community for the wildly successful iPhone: at the same time, the growth of Google's Android operating system represents an open-source competitor gaining traction and thereby widening the pool of potential participants in app communities for both public and private platforms and usages.[9]

Such tensions between proprietary and open-source operating systems notwithstanding the logic of openness and empowerment in the private realm attracted attention from observers in government, notably the aforementioned, former US federal government CIO, Vivek Kundra. While serving as CIO to the Washington, DC, authority, he oversaw what is believed to be the continent's first experimentation in "apps for democracy" by inviting citizens to develop new

---

[9] By contrast the rapid decline in app developers from Research in Motion products—notably Blackberries—is consistent and intertwined with this company's recent and ongoing struggles stemming from the displacement of the Blackberry by alternative mobile devices, notably Apple and Android smartphones and tablets.

service concepts to improve the quality of life of residents. Akin to the operating system platforms of private sector actors such as Apple, the Washington, DC, initiative would provide a basis for such user-centric mobilization—and a basis for making creative use of the data holdings in an unprecedented raw form. Such holdings, in combination with Web 2.0 tools and methodologies and data sources from elsewhere on the Internet, thereby enabled interested and capable residents to devise their own "apps" for showcasing and ultimately for widespread adoption across the community.[10]

Building upon the City of Edmonton's inaugural app competition within a Canadian jurisdiction, several municipalities joined forces and forged a group of four to promote wider open data efforts across the country, prodding the provincial and federal governments to follow suit (Giggey 2011). Internationally, the UK, the US, and Japan are regarded as public sector pioneers of the open data movement, the American context featuring the aforementioned local app contests in Washington, DC, and the Obama Administration's early usage of the "recovery.gov" platform discussed at the outset of this chapter.

The British experience is underscored by the following: first, the critical work of a Parliamentary Committee in 2012 already having reviewed various initiatives and provided recommendations in kind[11] and, secondly, the creation in London of the Open Data Institute[12] by leading Internet authorities seeking to deepen such efforts in the UK and around the world. As open data spreads around the world—consistent with the emergence of ubiquitous online data flows underpinned by cloud infrastructure systems and increasingly powerful mobile devices for individual users (Young 2012)—experiences thus far with public sector data releases underscore that the mere act of making data available is symbolically important but insufficient in driving participative public value creation (Helbig et al. 2012).

In sum, as openness becomes less a platform for data transparency and more a prism for the sorts of alternative and more participative governance mindsets in keeping with the advent of mobility, new governance capacities are required both culturally and structurally. Efforts to create such new capacities can be expected to encounter resistance due to the like-minded ownership tensions discussed throughout this chapter (as well as interrelated political tensions in terms of the organization and conduct of democracy, a thematic focus of later chapters). Another important variable is how governments interact with a technology industry itself dealing with similar sets of tensions between proprietary and open-source offerings.

---

[10] Source and additional details on the initiative: http://www.appsfordemocracy.org/

[11] The report provides a number of thoughtfully critical observations and recommendations pertaining to the early challenges encountered of releasing open data as well as improvements and reforms necessary in moving ahead. The report is available online: http://www.publications.parliament.uk/pa/cm201213/cmselect/cmpubacc/102/102.pdf

[12] Http://www.theodi.org

Procurement and Performance

Apple cofounder, Steve Wozniak, once famously quipped that one should "never trust a computer you cannot throw out the window." Cloud computing inverts this logic entirely: today's laptop and tablet devices can be purchased for evermore affordable prices with considerably expanded functionality and memory available via online connectedness (i.e., the cloud). This important shift presents a new paradigm for the individual in terms of shifting behavior and a willingness to trust computer system based—increasingly in terms of what matters, less within the actual devices and computers and more across a virtualized environment. This shift is no less profound and complex for governments, with important repercussions for procurement policies and mechanisms that ultimately shape the foundations of government's IT architecture.

Traditionally, governments have sought to procure their IT infrastructures through the purchasing of either off the shelf products and systems or customized alternatives, their commonality being that government sought ownership over the main infrastructure components (and most especially sought to maintain control over the data holdings housed across such components). Outsourcing arrangements between government and private sector partners gradually altered this approach by relying instead on a proprietary system provided by a private supplier: prior to the advent of the Internet and the cloud, this externalization applied mainly to hardware and software infrastructures, whereas data management and storage systems often remained internalized (even as they were purchased from outside vendors).

Such bilateral relationships across sectors have been highly contractual in efforts to mitigate risk and contain costs, thereby minimizing flexibility and collaboration: proprietary restrictions around intellectual property further reinforced such tendencies (Langford and Roy 2008, 2009). Governments have thus embraced outsourcing relationships to varying degrees depending on their willingness to cede control and infrastructure ownership to an external partner and the according payoff in doing so relative to insourced options where government builds and maintains the infrastructure itself (ibid.).

Cloud-based infrastructures, however, invariably deepen reliance on more open and shared forms of infrastructure that are neither owned by government nor directly underpinned by bilateral contracts with private vendors offering (mainly) proprietary solutions. As the previously noted 2011 British Parliamentary Report (*Recipe for Rip-Off*) effectively underscores, if government is to become more agile, innovative procurement methodologies featuring a much greater emphasis on openness (in turn a key feature of cloud systems) will be required. The following quote from this British review is thus indicative of how social media platforms external to governments—examples of cloud computing in their own right—can reshape internal IT infrastructure and the sorts of investments and choices made by the public sector:

> Facebook emphasised "the value of creating a web environment that is structured by building specialized applications on an open platform". One of the major advantages of an open platform model is the entrepreneurship and flexibility it fosters. As the basic structure of the

website is open for development, companies and public agencies can call on a wide variety of web expertise to create the more specialised applications, features, or tools required to suit specific needs.

We see a clear opportunity for Government to adopt this model. IT enabled public services should be provided on an open platform with open interfaces. Government should provide the necessary open infrastructure that empowers people inside and outside of Government to innovate. Making this happen will be part of the transition we have mentioned above from an organisation-centric view of public services to one based on the needs of the citizen. (p. 9, Public Administration Committee, British House of Commons 2011)

This type of political discourse is important in fostering greater sensitivity and learning for stakeholders both within and outside of government as to the shifting contours of procurement. The classic model of government specifying and contracting in advance its precise needs—as well as traditional outsourcing models to select vendors through highly proprietary and secretive contracts—is giving way to new approaches predicated on wider communities of participants including developers both large and small (Eaves 2009). Governments are beginning to recognize greater incentives to encourage such openness—both as a strategic consumer of technology and as a promoter of innovation in society more broadly (ibid.).

Indeed, governments must also guard against misnomers such as claims that cloud systems simply displace entirely the need for procurement systems. While certain cloud offerings are freely and readily available online, the embracement of enterprise platforms and infrastructure components via cloud solutions calls for careful analysis and an in-house capacity for appreciating and assessing cloud options and their wider governance implications. Instead of displacing procurement, then, cloud solutions significantly alter procurement processes and challenge governments to balance government-wide coordination with flexibility and choice.

The novel shift in mindset here is that the procurement of cloud tools and solutions is less about centrally purchasing and imposing customized projects on the entire government (as per the aforementioned South African example) and more about coordinating the facilitation of open and certified standards for the government as a whole. Across this latter template, individualized units can remain empowered to make informed and optimal choices that balance centralized efficiency and collaborative innovation (in contrast to the imposition of outsourced or internalized proprietary solutions on all government entities irrespective of size, scope, and governance specificities).

More About New Capacities Than Lower Costs

Overall, findings from a comprehensive global survey on cloud computing deployments suggest that while cost savings are important, they are not the key driver for the deployment of cloud systems (CSC 2011). Rather, the growing need for new and more agile capacities—with both flexibility and security tied to the growing use of mobile devices—is the most predominant reason for pursuing cloud options, with cost savings realized to date at only extremely modest levels.

Such findings underscore the need for sobriety with regards to expectations and planning. Much like previous era of large-scale IT outsourcing, there is a tendency for technology enthusiasts (from both government and industry, each with their own incentives to do so, especially in today's economic and fiscal environment) to want to frame investments in new IT systems as a means of cost savings, despite the fact that experience suggests that large-scale savings are rarely if ever achieved (OECD 2001; Collier 2011). This is not to say that greater efficiency is not a laudable goal. The summation of a small number of savings-generating initiatives can become significant, and there is some early documented research by the private sector quantifying environmental benefits that provide additional benefit streams (Accenture 2009). Yet the combination of up-front investment and transitional cost means that massive short-term savings are an unrealistic rationale for any new IT investment—and cloud computing is unlikely to prove to be an exception to this rule.

In addition, even in the private sector where cloud computing adoption is generally more widespread and advanced, concerns around security persist—denoting an important consideration for many companies. These findings reinforce the ongoing implications of the discussion above surrounding the degree to which cloud computing is an enhancer of security or one that potentially reveals new weaknesses. In the public sector, where the safeguarding of personal information in critical fields such as health and environmental and public safety is paramount, these discussions surrounding security are likely to remain crucial factors in the cloud computing conversation for some time to come. The following passage underscores the centrality of this data security issue:

> In spite of the overall satisfaction of current cloud users and the number of companies that are considering adopting cloud services, there are still concerns that limit the growth of cloud computing. The issues that continue to create anxiety revolve around data security, privacy and the physical location of the data.

> Because of these concerns, the vast majority of companies surveyed do not intend to move employee or customer information and accounts or financial data services to the cloud in the foreseeable future. Furthermore, regarding the location of data, companies feel more confident if their data is stored locally or nationally, as they are concerned about the potential impact of another country's laws on data storage. It appears companies are more confident when data is maintained in their home country where the laws and legal system are familiar... Cloud computing customers do want value, but the savings should come from the hardware and redundant storage side of the equation, not at the expense of confidence and security. (p. 1, de Jong 2011)

In sum, government efforts aimed at exploring and ultimately embracing cloud computing require careful consideration of both cost and capacity issues within a wider and fluid societal lens of openness and ownership. At the same time, central to the evolution of the cloud in terms of performance and accountability are complex concerns and challenges pertaining to security—of the infrastructure and the data flows processed upon it, the focus of the next chapter and the one following it.

Chapter 5
Cybersecurity

Systemic Vulnerability

The Internet facilitates a level of interoperability among individuals, organizations, sectors, and countries that generates widening opportunities for collaboration and innovation—central themes of the preceding chapters. Digital infrastructure is rapidly becoming the lifeblood of a more virtual and interdependent globalizing economy, as every major industrial sector widens its reliance on electronic systems and online connectivity—from power generation and supply to finance and manufacturing. Furthermore, the previous chapter describes the ascent of cloud computing as a shared ownership model of networked and interoperable computing systems for data storage and management internally—as well as frontend usage of online programs and social media platforms by users enjoined with more powerful and more mobile processing and communication devices.

At the same time, online and virtual threats to organizations in all sectors have become a way of life: one American survey undertaken in 2011, for instance, reported 100 % coverage of respondent organizations dealing with some form of cyber-breach or attack either from internal or external sources (Ponemon 2011a, b). Many observers estimate the total cost of damages related to cyber-crime up to now having surpassed one trillion dollars annually, with the private security industry expected to surpass $80 billion in annual revenues by the year 2017 (ibid.). Despite significant and highly public breaches involving companies such as Citigroup, Sony, LinkedIn, and many others, some outside of the private sector suspect the security industry itself of bolstering such figures and implied threats. Others insist that such figures may underplay the problem since few companies are keen to divulge breaches and weaknesses and many individuals may unknowingly be victimized.

Facing increasingly frequent threats externally, governments carry the dual responsibilities of safeguarding their own infrastructures and information holdings as well as overseeing the digital resilience of their jurisdictions as a whole (Quigley and Roy 2011). Such public sector challenges were underscored in Canada in late 2012

J. Roy, *From Machinery to Mobility: Government and Democracy in a Participative Age*, Public Administration and Information Technology 2, DOI 10.1007/978-1-4614-7221-6_5, © Springer Science+Business Media New York 2013

and early 2013 by an Auditor General's scathing review of the federal government's cybersecurity efforts on the one hand and a massive loss of personal data just a few months later on the other hand.[1]

Openness and Interdependence

As greater openness and mobility bring heightened interdependence, the importance of cybersecurity deepens for both governments and all of society. For individuals, the challenge lies in establishing and maintaining trusted and secure identities for conversations and transactions while mitigating intentional and unintentional risks—and deciding for oneself the appropriate trade-offs between privacy and openness. Organizations must foster strategies and systems in order to safeguard information assets and infrastructure in a world of ubiquitous Internet access and multiplying devices (and thus access points) linking employees within an ever-more densely networked and mobile set of stakeholders. Societies collectively must balance the collective benefits of openness with the systemic vulnerabilities that flow from such openness. The Obama Administration's Cyberspace Policy Review stated in 2009 that: "Threats to cyberspace pose one of the most serious economic and national security challenges of the twenty-first century for the United States and our allies" (p. 8, Goodyear et al. 2010). Accordingly, then, governments must address cybersecurity as both an internal challenge and one encompassing of all such levels within their jurisdiction.

How best to do so entails judgments pertaining to the contrasting prospects of open-source and proprietary systems reviewed in the previous chapter. In other words, due in large part to the collective attributes of open-sourced systems underpinning the notion of the cloud, whether a more online and open world is a more dangerous one is itself an inherently contested notion. Proponents of transparency and open sourcing espouse the collective resilience and intelligence of post-proprietary governance (i.e., open source) where theoretically, everyone is a potential defender and contributor to safeguarding against unforeseen weaknesses as well as more malicious threats. Skeptics worry that such openness augments vulnerabilities.

In his presentation of eight fundamental elements to workable and effective cloud computing systems, Wyld's emphasis on universality and openness—along with security and privacy—underscores the competing forced at hand (Wyld 2010a, b).

---

[1]The data breach involved the loss of an external memory stick within the federal department responsible for student loan processing (Human Resources and Skills Development Canada): financial and personal data on an estimated 500,000 citizens, holders of student loans, was said to be misplaced. One irony of this episode is reporting that the spectre of legal action against the government may prompt it toward wider usage of cloud systems—for which the federal government has proved trepid in exploring due to concerns about data privacy (Press 2013). Such themes in terms of personal privacy and the Government of Canada's cautious temperament toward digital renewal and cloud systems specifically are returned to later in this chapter as well as Chap. 8, respectively.

The author offers two competing and somewhat contradictory predictions for the coming decade that further highlight the accumulating systemic stakes—both positive and negative: on the one hand, the democratization of technology from more open, online, and interoperable infrastructure is said to promise tremendous benefit to societies, whereas on the other hand, the author predicts two or three "massive" security breaches each year likely to galvanize media attention and public scrutiny (Wyld 2010a, b). Such pronouncements, while seemingly contradictory at times, underscore the duality of compounding opportunities and threats as cloud computing systems and expanding online activity further augment the degrees of interdependence across critical electronic systems in and across both industry and government.

Such competing logics also replicate themselves in terms of online information flows for new styles of openness in traditionally proprietary fields such as journalism and learning. The most visible example is perhaps Wikipedia and its displacement of hard form encyclopedia resources in a manner that enables the validity and accuracy of posted information to be vetted by society at large. The power of such instantaneous and collective mobilization can be both informational much as it can serve as an important determinant of spontaneous and collectivized trust.

One such tragic example came in 2010 when a Polish aircraft, carrying the country's President and numerous dignitaries, crashed in Russia en route to a bilateral ceremony with officials from both countries. Given the historical sensitivities of relations between both countries, this incident carried at least the potential for suspicion and conspiracy theories to arise, whereas any such risk was mitigated by the real-time online reporting of Wikipedia members that, in turn, provided a comprehensive and highly credible source of facts and opinions themselves subject to constant scrutiny and revision.[2]

The openness and learning that ensued can be partially credited as contributors to the thoughtful manner by which both countries addressed the cause and aftermath of this tragic accident. One could point to a somewhat analogous relationship between the Polish tragedy and Microsoft's evolution in recent years—namely, the reduced scope for cynicism and outright conspiracy theorizing in an environment of collective openness. In the former case, the extensive and real-time reporting of what transpired (as well as the timely and sincere response by Russian authorities) mitigated what, in a pre-Internet era, may well have served as fertile ground for suspicion and accusation across at least portions of the impacted societies.

Consequently, participative openness can buttress the traditional mantra that secrecy breeds suspicion. Yet notwithstanding such examples, there remains much about the Internet and online activity that remains in the shadows—shielded inadvertently or intentionally from public viewing and understanding.

The US Government's efforts are emblematic in this regard. Much as 9–11 drove a fundamental restructuring of air transportation infrastructure and government's security apparatus for addressing terrorist threats during the Bush Administrations,

---

[2] Source. Wikipedia: http://en.wikipedia.org/wiki/2010_Polish_Air_Force_Tu-154_crash

the arrival of President Obama in 2008 would signal a similarly important inflection point in terms of prioritizing cyber-efforts in both reactive and proactive manners.

The absence of a crystallizing event such as the 9–11 attacks nonetheless alters the political landscape—bringing less sharpened demands for clarity of action. By the same token, however, the accentuated emphasis on secrecy and covertness that gained traction in the previous decade remains a key variable (and a source of friction between Obama's campaign pledges for more institutional openness and the realities of governing that ensued). In short, the struggles and efforts of the Obama Administration are an important reference point (and source of influence) for all democracies, most especially neighboring Canada, and as such, they are examined at some length in this chapter.

The Search for Hybrid Governance[3]

Within the US and across much of the world, there is growing recognition that cybersecurity requires innovative responses that must be facilitated more than ordained by public sector authorities. Such is the imperative of hybrid governance models—which challenge governments to both organize and behave in new ways less constrained by machinery-laden models of bureaucracy and control and more outward and participative (and thus aligned with mobility).

Meaningful and effective hybrid governance must reconcile four competing and complex realities. Firstly, President Obama and other political and industry leaders around the world have sought to create attention and dialogue on the risks of cybersecurity to an unprecedented degree—galvanizing awareness and action within and outside of government. Secondly, the internalizing of public sector action is closely interrelated with bureaucratic structures and mindsets emphasizing secrecy and hierarchical control. Thirdly, the private sector is a key player—as owner and operator of major portions of critical telecommunication infrastructure and electronic online systems: while markets can generate innovation to mitigate cybersecurity risks, competitive and proprietary concerns often limit information sharing and concerted action. Fourthly, consistent with the nature of online space and activity and many emerging cyber-threats (Cornish 2009), there may be merit (and indeed necessity) in looking to hybrid arrangements that include more organic and unconventional governance mechanisms and strategies (of the sort that are consistent with a Web 2.0 ethos and underpinning many of the threat movements requiring attention and response).

With respect to the first point, President Obama sought to instill a prism of leadership and accountability at the highest level:

---

[3] Significant portions of this section are largely drawn from the following article: Quigley, K., & Roy, J. (2011). Cyber-security and risk management in an interoperable world: An examination of Governmental Action in North America. *Social Sciences Computer Review, 30*(1), 83–94.

> My administration will pursue a new, comprehensive approach to securing America's digital infrastructure. This new approach starts at the top with this commitment from me: from now on, our digital infrastructure, the networks and computers we depend on every day, will be treated as they should be—as a strategic national asset. Protecting this infrastructure will be a national security priority. We will ensure these networks are secure, trustworthy and resilient.[4]

Such executive branch backing can underpin new organizational capacities designated as vehicles for more holistic coordination. Indeed, two important benefits can emerge from hierarchical leadership and direction setting: firstly, a willingness and ongoing efforts to both measure and report on progress in a public manner (and also via Congressional and Parliamentary bodies as the public's first line of accountability) and, secondly, in sparking and accelerating a public dialogue on a critical issue such as cybersecurity that otherwise remains poorly understood and thus poorly suited to social learning and collective intelligence, a basis for more enlightened governance and policy systems.

While the Obama Administration is ripe with tensions between traditional bureaucracy and new governance capacities (and related strains of secrecy versus openness[5]), the executive leadership brought to this issue has nonetheless rendered it more visible and more widely examined in both technocratic and political realms. The Canadian case by contrast is notable for the absence of clear political commitment and open debate with respect to cyber-matters specifically. The resulting mindset pertaining to cyber and other forms of critical infrastructure is a reinforcement of a secretive and hierarchist mindset of governmental authorities, most especially those at the federal level (Quigley and Roy 2011). A particular concern here is the absence of more open and robust mechanisms for sharing information between industry and government, a major issue given that the vast majority of critical infrastructure assets and systems are owned and operated by companies (Clemens and Crowley 2012). While the US has sought to heighten appreciation of the need to share information and create new hybrid capacities to do so (as described above), the lack of an open Canadian dialogue in this regard reinforces secrecy inside of government and covertness in its private sector dealings.

The absence of more robust action may be due to the lack of a crystallizing event (despite a growing catalogue of cyber-breaches in Canada, none have thus far resulted in widespread or highly visible damage) or the general decline of interest and prioritization in digital matters that has characterized the Harper Government. Widening concerns regarding such complacency were highlighted in June 2012 by

---

[4]Obama, B. (2009). *Obama announces complete overhaul of cyber security (Part 1)*, May 29th (http://www.youtube.com/watch?v=dgDsXAykAm0).

[5]The United States also reportedly launched its first major cyber-attack on another country in 2011, a coordinated effort with Israel aimed at destabilizing Iran's nuclear development program. The action, reported in the New York Times and in a subsequent book, also sparked heightened debate and concern among lawmakers about leaks and the need for secrecy pertaining to national security measures (yet another example of widening tensions between openness—imposed or invited—and the traditional public sector culture of secrecy).

the somewhat surprising release of an internal memo (through an access to information request of several months prior) prepared by the Canadian Deputy Minister (i.e., appointed Department Head) responsible for public safety for his Minister— lamenting Canada's vulnerability to cyber-attacks (ibid.; Mayeda and Miller 2012).

An October 2012 report by the Auditor General further criticized federal government efforts, exposing systemic weaknesses and the absence of the sort of political leadership and public engagement of the sort on display in recent years in the US. Moreover, as noted in the introduction of this book, a 2011 related effort by the federal government to permit an expansion of online surveillance by policing and security authorities sparked a major online backlash leading to a government retreat, an episode suggesting a lack of political and societal learning and nuance. Indeed, the framing of the proposed legislation as an attempt to better protect children online from predators was widely viewed as a massive political simplification designed to thwart any political opposition to the measures, a miscalculation likely contributing to the Government's trepid stance on cyber-security matters more generally (and one that further underscores the absence of a wider political dialogue on such matters).

The Obama Administration's 2009 Cyberspace Policy Review, by contrast, highlights the need for a national dialogue involving government, industry, and the public at large—emphasizing the need for coordinated action across all levels of government as well as across sectors (Goodyear et al. 2010). At the same time, reflecting the largely bureaucratic ethos of government, leadership and responsibility are centralized within the confines of the White House and the new Presidential, cybersecurity appointee. Here we witness clashes between vertical and horizontal lines of accountability: government understanding that it cannot act alone but nonetheless driven by conflicting pressures to act unilaterally and collaboratively. Within governments, these pressures play out within and between specific units and their leaders; across sectors they reflect government's dual role of orchestrating processes for inter-sectoral coordination and dialogue on the one hand and regulating and policing wherever necessary on the other hand.

In terms of this latter point, the hierarchical orientation of government authorities and a public interest orientation that often necessitates a guardian role is one that may coexist uneasily with the more competitive and individualist tendencies of the marketplace and industry actors. The overarching challenge, then, lies in finding innovative ways to expand government's role in an intelligent, agile, and adaptive manner—balancing state and market capacities in recognition of the fact that it is unlikely to be governments themselves that create the tools and mechanisms necessary to ensure a safe and resilient digital infrastructure but instead (1) ideas stemming from innovation and experimentation within the marketplace and (2) an alignment of public and private interests via collaborative efforts between both sectors. A key challenge here is that government alone cannot initiate collective action within the marketplace nor shape behavior in those dimensions of civil society with individualist or egalitarian tendencies and values.

Growing calls for industry self-reporting and self-monitoring are thus important in mobilizing market-based assessments of risk—and reactions to such assessments.

Accordingly, the Intelligence and National Security Alliance (2009) provided a thoughtful analysis of public–private partnering in a variety of contexts—with the aim of devising a suitable framework for sectoral collaboration specifically in the cybersecurity realm. As a point of departure for high-level guidance, they propose two fundamental dimensions to such an undertaking:

- An executive committee composed of representatives from individual, business and government organizations referred to here as a Cyber Security Panel, which represents the interests of businesses and individual users.
- A partner government organization responsible for some oversight, regulation and enforcement, focused on net security. Government is essential because only government has the authority and ability to fully investigate cyber incidents that may occur across networks and only government has the ability and legitimacy to regulate industry where private citizens' interests are at risk (as with privacy). (p. 4, INSA 2009)

This type of high-level collaboration—formalized in such a manner—is important in signalling the necessity of sectoral collaboration. Further, such a forum could bring to light the significant shared externalities of firms and industries—transforming the "widespread agreement that this long-term trend of grabbing the economic gains from information technology advances and ignoring their security costs has reached a crisis" (Goldsmith and Hathaway 2010) into concrete proactive measures and better planning for emergency preparedness and responses to incidents when they occur.

Yet in order to proceed in such a manner, governments must pursue strategies that facilitate multi-organizational collaboration while at the same time account for the competitive context of markets. Public authorities must recognize the disincentives that will constrain industry's willingness to share proprietary information (Langford and Roy 2009). It is unlikely industry will share information about their vulnerabilities: liability issues and concerns about brand and reputation are important vices here. Sector level forums can thus agree to certain levels of confidentiality provisioning where essential and necessary, while also facilitating participation in more open mechanisms for public and private dialogue that are necessary to build trust and expand information sharing. Shaping the mindset of markets in terms of expectations and incentives is particularly important, especially as evidence points to a strengthening correlation between cyber-vulnerabilities and a loss of shareholder value (Andoh-Baidoo et al. 2010).

This emphasis on transparency and openness can also be an important linkage to alternative governance formations which are more organic and communitarian in focus and orientation—and skeptical of industry and government capacities (especially existing ones). Such actors may be more open to the formation of new communities, akin to the self-governance dynamic becoming so prevalent in an online, interconnected world (Shirky 2008). Consistent with embracing the growing reach and prowess of Web 2.0 and social networking sites outside of government (Eggers 2005; Williams 2012; Wyld 2007) and the more networked democratic ethos taking hold (Stoker 2005; Roy 2008, 2010), the imperative facing public sector authorities is to forge innovative mechanisms for collective outreach and engagement.

Such mobilization can then align governmental authority with new collaborative capacities via communities and movements devoted to fostering greater collective security online—as well as shared reactive response capacities for breaches and breakdowns when they occur. One like-minded suggestion—attempting in some manner to align and link governmental authority with a more grassroots, spontaneous form of extended community—is offered by Irvine and Palmer (2010) in their proposed blueprint of a Cyber National Guard (in the United States although the authors acknowledge and endorse the need for an international capacity for this type of mechanism). Responding to the Obama Administration's Cyber Space Policy review that calls for new processes over the midterm between the government and the private sector to "assist in preventing, detecting, and responding to cyber-incidents," the notion of a Cyber National Guard is one of networked resilience through public funding and leadership coupled with private support and assistance—and driven by voluntary engagement and a communitarian-type ethos to both reactive and proactive forms of mobilization (ibid.).

The authors suggest, for example, such a body could greatly assist public awareness and education efforts, an approach that can to some degree marry the experimentalism of fatalists with an egalitarian-minded emphasis on shared preparation and building a culture of "cyber hygiene" (p. 59). Key here is government's willingness and ability to share authority in a manner that acknowledges the necessity of beyond traditional state and bureaucratic capacities. The creation of a US Cyber Challenge—a nationwide talent search to mobilize and nurture a cadre of 10,000 young Americans with cybersecurity skills—is a useful example of this type of grassroots initiative encouraged by government but working outside of the strict confines of public sector (Gupta 2010). Destabilized by recent breaches and attacks, a similarly inspired initiative in South Korea (labelled "the best of the best") has sought to leverage a grassroots culture of hacking toward bolstering the country's cyber-defenses against external threats, notably its northern neighbor (Kwon 2012).

Looking to such alternative and more collaborative and open governance movements can assist and accompany industry and government efforts to foster new outreach capacities more aligned with the networked realities of the Internet itself. Such governance experimentation is critically important in terms of both proactive preparation and mitigating the sorts of threats emerging in cyberspace. It is only by way of such hybrid strategies that governments can respond, both proactively and reactively, to the multifaceted risks of an evermore digitally and socially networked world. While straining the traditional governmental paradigm of bureaucracy and the traditional proprietary orientation of the marketplace, hybrid strategies carry the potential to better align a smarter and more strategic public sector role with the increasingly networked and diffuse realities of the mobility era.

Beyond Complacency: Employee and Public Engagement

An important element in the facilitation of new hybrid strategies for collective security (strategies that must invariably draw upon characteristics of adaptive governance and openness discussed in the preceding chapters) is widened public awareness and engagement in order to foster collective learning and resilience while also providing a degree of oversight and accountability of public sector efforts to combat threats. Nevertheless, the systemic secrecy of a traditional bureaucratic mindset can stymie such openness, creating now-familiar tensions between machinery and mobility.

Moreover, the steady and interrelated expansion of cloud computing, social media, mobile smart devices, and wireless Internet access creates a set of conditions ripe for inadvertent and malicious exploitation by an increasingly online public that is worrisomely passive and ill informed in the main with respect to online security and personal behavior (Ponemon 2011a, b). Even as openness and alternative ownership models and mindsets drive the formation of novel and more participative governance schemes, the steady expansion of cloud platforms and mobile devices can also further augment the shared risks and consequences of cyber-insecurity. A 2012 US federal digital government strategy, for example, outlines the heightened vulnerability:

> Mobile devices have unique security challenges. Due to their portability, they are easy to misplace, potentially compromising any unencrypted sensitive data or applications stored locally…The rate of change of mobile operating systems, new update and notification capabilities from external hardware and software vendors, diversity of the devices themselves, and introduction of employee-owned devices (BYOD) also make security in the mobile space more challenging than in a traditional desktop environment and require new approaches to continuously monitor and manage devices and secure the data itself.[6]

For public sector organizations pursuing mobility as an organizational mindset as well as technological strategy, an emphasis on employee awareness and responsibility is therefore central to fostering collective capacities for cybersecurity across infrastructure (including cloud systems and the myriad of personal devices deployed by public servants within and outside of the organization's physical and virtual walls) and data processing. As a retired American Lieutenant General describes it,

> Mobile users are looking for ease of access and speed of use, but are assuming security and privacy. This requires a very different "corporate" security approach. As organizations integrate new technologies and IT systems expand into the cloud, cyber-security must adapt to address the expectations of users. "The future of cyber-security is sustainable risk management," said Lt. Gen. Raduege. "The tipping point of cyber will likely come when it blends in seamlessly with the agency's broader business portfolio and becomes part of how the agency operates and delivers on its mission." That calls for a new cultural approach that's integrated into almost every aspect of public and private life he noted. "People will compare trade-offs and make tough choices based on data from a real-time view of the cyber landscape (p. 1, Raduege 2011)."

---

[6]Source, US White House. (2012). *Digital government: Building a 21st century platform to better serve the American people* (http://www.whitehoiuse.gov/sites/default/files/omb/egov/digital-government/digital-government.html). The report provides a thoughtful and useful examination of the implications of mobility and security for public sector governance both internally and in terms of external outreach.

Importantly, while this call for sustainable risk management as a new organizational ethos underscores individual choices and decisions, such an enlightened culture must also emphasize responsibility. As the passage also implies, such enlightenment also implies a greater overlap and blending of formerly separate public and private realms, one consistent with the evolution of work patterns and organizational governance examined in earlier chapters.

Cybersecurity thus reinforces a now-familiar set of tensions. A machinery-laden, bureaucratic orientation of government primarily treats public servants as specialized workers to be assigned and overviewed within strict temporal and physical employment settings. By contrast, a more dispersed and multilayered mobile environment blurs such boundaries—creating new opportunities for empowerment but also a new imperative for framing and pursuing cybersecurity both individually and collectively through a shared set of expectations and responsibilities that become the basis for regularized learning and accountability. In other words, any effective and resilient security ethos requires proactive engagement and participation across all levels of organizations as well as across society at large.

Central to such an evolution are complex and interrelated matters of trust—as well as fluid viewpoints and behavioral values pertaining to privacy and the safeguarding and usage and sharing of personal information. The emergence of online—and more recently mobile commerce and related forms of payment—bring together systemic conditions for cybersecurity and the public sector role examined in this chapter with the wider set of choices made by individuals as both consumers and citizens (and potentially as activists as well). These latter choices, within the shifting and interrelated realms of payments and privacy, constitute the central focus of the next chapter.

Chapter 6
Payments and Privacy

Virtual Channels and Trust

Electronic commerce is owed to a dynamic of competitive openness about product and service information on the one hand and the efficiency and convenience of transacting online on the other hand. The first point often distinguishes private sector offerings from those of government (where there is less competition due to the nature of public goods and services), whereas the latter enjoins both sectors in important ways such as the basic enabling requirement of cybersecurity. Separately and collectively, all organizations seeking to leverage Internet platforms and channels must devise secure mechanisms for facilitating monetary transactions—and by implication, storing and processing personal and confidential information.

The central nexus between online security and trust explains the multichannel realities of service architectures in both sectors. With respect to online commerce, confidence in online mechanisms for transacting payment and product and service information is essential. Traditional retail and in-person service delivery methods may still entail an electronic transaction at the point of sale—a debit or credit card purchase, for example, or instead a reliance on more traditional, tangible forms of paper and coin currencies as a means of exchange. The emergence of the so-called digital wallet, examined further below, is meant to blur such distinctions given the steady expansion of mobile devices, namely, smartphones and tablets.

In government, as noted, many service transactions are typically less frequent and more routine. Yet for those who may still shun online channels due to inability or discomfort, governments often face a wider set of political and organizational complexities than private companies. In the marketplace, it is mainly a matter of personal preference and choice, whereas in the government realm, research demonstrates that individual dealings between citizens and governments off-line reflect a greater level of service consumption on the part of those citizens—often due to disadvantaged socioeconomic status or uniquely demanding events and circumstances (Dutil et al. 2010; Lips 2012).

J. Roy, *From Machinery to Mobility: Government and Democracy in a Participative Age*, Public Administration and Information Technology 2, DOI 10.1007/978-1-4614-7221-6_6, © Springer Science+Business Media New York 2013

Globally, the advent of electronic payments and transfers in more readily available and affordable forms is said to create new opportunities for empowering wider segments of society to generate and transfer wealth, thereby a basis for reducing socioeconomic and digital divide (an opportunity highlighted by the United Nations 2012 Global E-Government Review). Within the most widely digitized countries, by contrast, what is notable is the greatly reduced digital divide as the Internet has become nearly ubiquitous—and governments, in turn, are able to dramatically lessen their reliance on paper-based forms and currencies.

The current e-government strategy in Denmark, for example, builds on preceding efforts in that country to lessen the usage of paper-based cheques to citizens and companies and to realize fully virtualized interactions between the citizenry and the state over the next few years:

> The central aim of the strategy is that by 2015 digital self-service solutions will be established as the normal way for citizens to interact with the public sector. The new strategy, called "The digital path to future welfare," aims to phase out paper-based forms and postage.[1]

In both of these developing and developed world examples, the commonality of rising mobility is a key determinant. Mobile banking in Denmark has thus emerged more rapidly, finding widespread adoption in a manner reflective of the open source and participative dynamics examined in earlier chapters:

> In 2010, the Danske Bank Group delivered a number of new solutions for customers that put us at the forefront of the efforts to make it quick and easy to do your banking. In September we were the first bank in Denmark to launch mobile banking for smartphones. The timing proved to be right on target. So far, across the Group, the application has been downloaded more than 160,000 times…We have just begun an initiative in which users can propose mobile banking features that they would like us to develop. (p. 5, Danske Bank 2011)

The closing line of this passage invokes the participatory dynamic of application development first examined in Chap. 4, an example of mobility and openness aligning itself in some manner with what remains a proprietary infrastructure of a private financial institution. At the same time, it bears underlining that deeper levels of collaboration and interoperability between the private and public sectors than is the case in most countries explain not only this rapid mobile rollout of banking tools but also the richer and more advanced ecosystem for service and payment offerings enjoining both sectors and the Danish citizenry (Roy 2006; Blakemore and Lloyd 2007).

---

[1] The strategy further explains: "Citizens will use the Internet for all applications and notifications to the public sector, namely, a moving notification; the enrolment of a child in a nursery; or when issuing a new passport. In addition, all citizens and businesses will automatically be given a free digital mailbox to which all communications from the public sector will be sent. The transition will take place gradually, as user-friendly eGovernment solutions are introduced in increasingly more areas. Help will be available for citizens who find it hard to use the new solutions. By 2015, the Government expects to be able to send 80 % of all correspondence to citizens in digital form. It is also expected that 80 % of all applications and correspondence from citizens will be in digital form." Source: http://www.epractice.eu/en/document/288205

A related example of processing taxation is further illustrative of the relationship between transparency, trust, and virtualization. In Denmark, as in all Scandinavian countries, tax returns are pre-completed by the tax authority before delivery to citizens who, in turn, have the option of modification or simply confirming its completeness virtually (notably and in a unique example of unfettered openness and transparency, neighboring Norway makes available online the completed returns of every citizen, a policy garnering both support and controversy). In many Danish municipalities, access to this service and most others provided by any level of public sector authority in the country is facilitated by a single online identity verification mechanism providing a virtual portal into this integrative scheme (Reinwald and Kraemmergaard 2011).

In Canada, by contrast, although two-thirds of citizens filing tax returns did so online in 2012, the usage of paper remains widespread as both a means of filing and a basis for preparation and processing (as various income and expenditure sources require the gathering of appropriate documentation from various parties, i.e., employer, financial institutions, charities, etc.). Moreover, despite growing efforts to align and integrate specific service offerings, companies and citizens in Canada remain largely responsible for navigating separate tax and regulatory processes across local, provincial, and federal governments that vary in terms of their usage of electronic and more traditional delivery channels (Reddick and Roy 2013).

The contrast between Canada and Scandinavia underscores two important differences that are central to the duration of this chapter: firstly, the more engrained multichannel realities of the former and a continued reliance on paper and, secondly, significant variances in public perceptions and values pertaining to personal privacy and the handling and sharing of personal information across organizational and sectoral boundaries. It is the unique and virtuous coexistence of transparency and trust in both digital infrastructure and public institutions more widely that explains the digital leadership of Scandinavian nations (reflecting their status at the top of rankings such as the UN Global Index) and the more rapid embracement of virtual processes and online activities that has resulted within society and in terms of digital government efforts (Reinwald and Kraemmergaard 2011).[2]

For much of the rest of the world, any drive to more seamless and paperless payment and processing mechanisms is more complex and contested. The United Kingdom, for instance, abandoned its plans to mandate the elimination of paper cheques usage by governments, the resulted considerable unease and uncertainly across portions of industry (notably small companies) and segments of society often associated with persisting digital and socio-economic divides that remain ongoing realities of most developed nations as well as the developing world, i.e., the elderly, disabled, poorly educated, etc. (Ashlie 2011).

---

[2]Details of the Danish e-government strategy from 2011 to 2015 (subtitled the "digital path to future welfare") are available online: http://www.digst.dk/da/Servicemenu/English/Policy-and-Strategy/~/media/Digitaliseringsstrategi/Engelsk_strategi_tilgaengelig.ashx

The crucial nexus between public trust and cybersecurity was evident in the UK experience:

> Public trust, consumer confidence and consumer protection are of paramount importance. In the UK, lobby groups with a consumer focus were vocal in their apprehension of the cheque elimination scheme. Letter writing campaigns from consumers and small charities won the day. For a new system to gain acceptance in Canada, its benefits need to be clear, issues around cyber security need to be addressed, and regulation needs to be effective and transparent. (p. 12, ibid.)

Such resistance and pushback suggest that for significant segments of the populous trust has yet to become fully virtualized—and that it may be some time, if ever, before complete virtualization is achieved. At the same time, however, the steady expansion of mobile devices such as smartphones and tablets implies a more digitized future—with more and more transactions and payments not only online but also portable and facilitated by expanding technological mobility. Such are the parameters for the emergence of mobile payments and any eventual realization of what's frequently described as "a digital wallet."

Mobile Payments

A 2011 study of American mobile shoppers reveals a mixed portrait of real progression and significant growth potential on the one hand and the centrality of security and privacy on the other hand. The main findings sketch out both the potential and hindrances to mobile commerce: for example, one in five smartphone owners already deploys their device as a virtual wallet in some manner (whereas 47 % of smartphone owners and 56 % of tablet owners, respectively, expressed their intentions to embrace mobile purchases); at the same time, data security and the novelty and uncertainty of the user experience are salient barriers for more than one-half of mobile device owners (Indvik 2011).

The Canadian mobile landscape is equally fertile—with similar shadows. One 2011 study, for example, revealed 44 % of Canadians owning a smartphone (outnumbering simple cellular, feature phones), with three-quarters of this group having already undertaken some form of purchase using their mobile device (Gooderham 2012). In 2012, furthermore, the Canadian Banker's Association published its industry guidelines for mobile payments, representing a key foundational plank for the expansion of such offerings and new partnerships between financial and technology companies.[3]

---

[3] In May 2012 CICB and Rogers announced a joint initiative for the country's first integrative mobile payment solution to be rolled out in a pilot basis. Details of this initiative are available online: http://www.newswire.ca/en/story/974935/cibc-and-rogers-unveil-the-future-of-mobile-payments-in-canada

Separately, in early 2013 RIM announced an agreement with VISA for a similarly inspired mobile payment platform involving Blackberry devices. Such examples are indicative of a growing movement that can be expected to accelerate in the coming years.

Such promise is nonetheless tempered by North American laggardness in terms of mobile banking (in comparison to other European and Asian jurisdictions), of usage by a small segment of the Canadian population (albeit one that is growing more rapidly than initial uptake levels of more traditional online channels[4]). It is reasonable to draw some analogous ties between government and banking. Whereas the Canadian Government became an early national champion of Internet infrastructure and government leveraging of online channels for service delivery, in recent years this progress and interest has waned, and mobile service delivery has yet to develop into a significant component of government's online presence. In contrast, then, to the aforementioned Scandinavian examples where close collaboration and concerted leadership by both sectors have facilitated a shared infrastructure for mobile identity authentication and transactions, a relatively uncoordinated set of strategies has characterized Canada in recent years (an issue returned to below).

Consequently, driven by this unrealized potential, the North American market features rising competition among alternative payment schemes predicated on mobility. Such schemes include not only traditional infrastructures of financial institutions and credit and debit cards but also alternative players such as Google and Apple targeting the widening nexus between technology, mobility, and payment. As one representative of PayPal Canada states, "there's a lot of people vying to be your wallet."[5]

The Canadian federal government responded to this complicating set of options and choices in 2011 with the formation of a task force to examine the domestic payment system, and its findings are instructive as to the scale of changes that lie ahead. The task force reported a high degree of disenchantment among consumers and industries with the status quo and urged government to undertake significant and aggressive actions to upgrade and refurbish the Canadian model. Central to this refurbishment is a reduced reliance on paper-based cheques that persists in Canada (an estimated one billion paper cheques written annually, with 60 % issues by governments and private corporations) and greater efforts to facilitate more widespread digital innovation in transaction and payment models such as new forms of digital wallets described above (Ashlie 2011).

As the Government of Canada contemplates its response (through 2012 and early 2013), its trepid pace in doing so coupled with its own limited usage of mobile service channels suggests a profile consistent with the limited action on cybersecurity observed in the previous chapter. Although 2011 and 2012 may be viewed as

---

[4]CIBC reported in 2012, for instance, faster growth in year one of mobile banking (in 2011) than in the initial year of online banking offerings during the 1990s.

[5]"Envision a digital wallet platform in which credit card, debit card, banking and other information becomes part of the smartphone itself, enabling consumers to make point-of-sale purchases. For example, 'contactless' or 'tap-and-go' systems using near-field communication (NFC), now popular on specialty cards at some retailers, will let customers pay by waving their phone in front of a point-of-sale terminal. Transactions can also be completed by short message service (SMS) or by quick response, or QR, codes." Source: http://www.theglobeandmail.com/globe-investor/personal-finance/financial-road-map/digital-wallet-slow-to-gain-acceptance/article2414790/?from=sec501

noteworthy years in public service reform—with the first Conservative majority budget promising significant workforce reductions—interest in digital reforms was mainly absent from government plans with the exception of a trepid open data strategy (following subnational and other national examples) and two additional examples pertaining to internal communications and travel and infrastructure consolidation, their commonality being an emphasis on cost savings.[6]

The relative laggardness of the Canadian Government with respect to digital payment reform externally and its own internal usage of mobility as a strategic platform may reflect an ideological preference for market-driven leadership in these domains.[7] With respect to payments specifically, government announcements in 2012 pertaining to a gradual and selective reduction in paper cheques by 2016 are thus notable in two respects: firstly, the framing of such a move as an efficiency driver and, secondly, the absence of mobile channels as a means to achieve this objective (the emphasis instead on existing forms of electronic payments, particularly direct deposit systems already in wide use). Any subsequent steps on both fronts are intertwined with matters pertaining to the virtualization of identity management.

Identity Management

The Canadian public sector's trepid pursuit of new identity management mechanisms that are the basis of more integrated online—and now increasingly mobile service offerings—is rooted in the set of both private and public governance complexities discussed above. For example, an interoperable framework encompassing public and private sectors could yield an integrated, electronic and portable identifier as a basis of a smart card for a range of commercial and governmental services. Such cards exist in numerous countries—including Belgium, where the initiative not only reflects public–private coordination but a high level of back-office, shared infrastructure across one of the world's most complex and often politically fragmented federations (Langford and Roy 2008; Schick 2011). The existence and usage of such a card, underpinned by a government registry (components of which

---

[6]Firstly, the 2012 federal budget speech included a pledge to explore the widespread adoption of "tele-presence" videoconferencing technologies as a basis for reduced travel and reliance on face-to-face meetings: thus an austerity-driven IT investment. Secondly, 2011 saw the creation of a new internal entity, Shared Services Canada (SSC), mandated to refurbish the internal digital infrastructure for the government as a whole—and such transfer elements of previously separate systems across departments and agencies into a single, centrally coordinated and shared model. The expectation is that SSC could eventually lead to the publication of a formal government strategy on cloud computing—of the sort that we see adopted by many other countries including the US and Canadian Westminster cousins, Australia, New Zealand, and the United Kingdom. SSC and the Government of Canada's digital priorities are further discussed in Chap. 8.

[7]Indeed, such an orientation is consistent with policies emphasizing greater competition and open investment domestically and internationally coupled with an austerity-driven fiscal stance imposing constraints on governmental programs and actions.

are typically outsourced to private sector companies), furthermore, replaces a national census survey since the relevant information is already gathered within the realm of the public sector.

Though indicative of many European and Asian jurisdictions, the Belgian model has not been transportable to Canada (or like-minded countries such as the US, UK, and Australia) for two interrelated reasons: firstly, the complexity and cost of constructing such an infrastructure and, secondly, the politics of privacy. In contrast to Belgium, then, the United States has sought a largely market-driven model by which the US federal government, under the auspices of the Obama Administration 2011 National Strategy for Trusted Identities in Cyberspace, has sought to indirectly orchestrate the creation of a framework of commonly recognized and increasingly open standards and protocols that can, in turn, facilitate transferability and seamlessness across sectors and government levels.

Prior to taking power in 2006, Canadian Prime Minister Harper and his Conservative Party had called for the creation of a national identity card (such an identifier does not exist in Canada where birth and vehicle registration as well as health-care transactions are provincial domains and the federal social insurance number had lacked comprehensiveness and security for wider usage beyond its role as primarily a basis for federal government programs and services). The impetus for Harper's pre-2006 vision had been 9-11 and like-minded efforts undertaken by British and Australian governments in the early part of that decade, along with heightened surveillance and data-gathering efforts on the part of American authorities (Roy 2006).

Despite mixed levels of support for such security-laden efforts, British and Australian populations would grow increasingly skittish in the face of debates pertaining to mandatory government identification schemes and the potential loss of privacy resulting. Similarly, a number of American incidents emerged pertaining to telephone and internet surveillance at the very least heightening sensitivity around such issues. In the British and Australian cases, such concerns along with rising cost estimates and doubts about the technological resilience of such systems were enough to lead both governments to abandon plans (and thus permit then-Prime Minister Harper to quietly set aside his own commitments in this regard).

Today, then, in the absence of more direct intervention by the federal government, the Canadian polity is characterized by a mosaic of varying provincial models. The Province of British Columbia, for example, has been the first to introduce an integrated public sector identifier capable of supplementing previously separate driver's license and health-care cards (though the optionality of this new card reflects privacy sensitivities politically, should citizen prefer to preserve such distinctions and thus silo-based usage of their personal information). The 2012 Ontario budget, passed acrimoniously within a minority legislature, would feature contested plans to privatize ServiceOntario as the lead service integrator for the province (and thus empowering such an entity to undertake new identity schemes, presumably in concert with private industry to exploit service and payment innovation opportunities).

The absence of an integrated, national identity scheme should not be viewed as inherently positive or negative, however—since different political cultures and governmental arrangements render such an option a different undertaking in each unique jurisdiction. Moreover, despite the uniquely cross-governmental example of Belgium (underpinned by wider levels of acceptance of government-held information than typically the case in the UK, Australia, and North America), there is considerable risk operationally in devising such a system in a top-down manner.

Yet at the same time, the advent of mobility accentuates fragmentation across not only government jurisdictions but between aspiring market-driven models competing to emerge. The considerable risk for the public sector in such an environment is the subsuming of matters of collective interest by interests and initiatives driven by commercial and customer service orientations. While some have traditionally argued that such an emphasis on individuality and choice is warranted in limiting the risks of a "big brother state" from emerging, such concerns must also be offset by the realities of ubiquitous data flows that now characterize modern life and the need for stronger forms of collective action.

A Widening Schism

In countries including Canada, the US, the UK, and Australia, the wider realization of mobile payment mechanisms is an endeavor fraught with much uncertainty and fragmentation, one likely to be driven by market-led innovations enjoining financial institutions, technology companies, and retailers both old and new. Even where a government administered solution may not be the answer, the absence of a clearer presence and orchestrating vision by government is important—as it risks accentuating existing digital divides between the roughly one-half of the population already gravitating to mobile channels via smart devices of one sort or another and the other half of the population (itself segmented between traditional online channels and paper and telephony-based transactions and interactions).

Such a cleavage is consistent with existing patterns of Internet infrastructure and access in these countries that are mainly determined by market forces (the notable exception being Australia's creation of a national crown corporation to ensure broadband connectivity across all rural and urban landscapes). A further distinction with Scandinavian comparators in this regard is the closer strategic relationship between the banking sector and government, an important driver of mobile infrastructure and payments and a partnership further underpinned by greater levels of digital literacy within government and across society.[8] Consistent with the discussion above pertaining to mobility and paperless payments, public concerns pertaining to privacy and information sharing are uniquely lower in these Northern European countries than anywhere else in the democratic world, an important factor

---

[8] This somewhat sweeping characterization would apply unevenly across the aforementioned countries but certainly applies to the Canadian scene for reasons discussed and in contrast to Scandinavian countries consistently rated by bodies such as the UN as global leaders in public sector digital deployment and societal connectivity and mobile devices.

in their leading digital performance since the inception of e-government (Roy 2006; Blakemore and Lloyd 2007).

By contrast, the implication for privacy matters in North America (and like-minded market-centric countries such as the UK and Australia) is an extension of an ethos of individualized choices and rights and a legalistic regime of rule enforcement and redress. Such an emphasis can only accentuate existing segmentation and divides as mobile channels and payment solutions are introduced and compete for advantage. In contrast to this customer and commercial orientation—or more accurately to complement it—there is a need for a richer and widened dialogue of citizen expectations and perspectives on the political and collective ramifications of digital life, particularly with respect to privacy and identity.

Privacy and "The Digital Self": Beyond the Customer Mindset[9]

A collective conundrum for societies embracing mobility and virtualization presents itself: a widening ethos of openness brings with it significant security vulnerabilities of the sort examined in the previous chapter (and thus clouding the emergence of mobile payments and processing systems). Yet it is also the limitations of such openness—bureaucratic and hierarchical mindsets of government coupled with a competitive and proprietary mentality of many companies in the marketplace—that result in greater secrecy or misinformation that stymies accountability and stunts collective learning and adaption.

The Internet has given rise to renewed and novel tensions between freedom and privacy, two terms that are often implicitly confused and at times fused as one in the same. Democratic governments have embraced the online world as a bastion of freedom and of information and liberalized action for the public (despite, at times, their own secretive nature). The mobilization of technology companies (albeit in a trepid and selective manner) and social media users against antidemocratic regimes coupled with alternative governance formations such as Anonymous further reinforces this mindset. Accordingly, so-called Anglo-Saxon countries – and to a lesser degree much of the OECD, have stymied efforts on the part of other parts of the world (notably China and Russia) to strengthen the guardian and regulatory functions of inter-governmental organizations such as the United Nations, fearing an erosion of this ethos of freedom that has largely personified the rise of online activity in the western world.

Privacy, therefore, has been viewed as a condition for such freedom—and thus often portrayed and conveyed to the public within these like-minded countries as an enshrined "right" to be upheld by government and commercial actors (except where government security and law enforcement agencies determine otherwise). The critical

---

[9] "The Digital Self" is the title of a 2011 book by Canadian journalist Nora Young (2012).

flaw with this approach has been in the passivity conveyed in this rights-based mentality—creating an expectation on the part of the public that privacy is a default and a near-guaranteed trait of participation in online life. Government service delivery agents thus promise such a guarantee as do financial institutions and other commercial agents routinely absorbing the cost of breaches that do occur (except in the most egregious acts of negligence or if there is malicious intent).

In addition, many countries (notably Westminster Parliamentary jurisdictions such as Canada and Australia) have established independent offices such as Privacy Commissioners in order to further reinforce such rights—and inadvertently a mindset of passiveness and protection—and importantly also to provide some level of transparency on both government and industry as to any potential erosion of such rights. In the United States, the role of Congressional oversight and investigative powers provides a similar role, especially pertaining to governmental action (albeit often via an uneasy alliance with Executive authorities pertaining to national security and defense matters; Bamford 2012).

The implicit treatment of the public in such a regime as that of a recipient of such guarantees is unhelpful and misleading on two counts: firstly, it fosters a false degree of confidence and complacency in the public domain in a virtual universe where vigilance and personal responsibility are called for; and secondly, the false predication put forth is that there is sufficient transparency in place over virtual data flows across state and market processes to warrant such confidence. The consequence is that trust in an online and increasingly mobile world is dependent upon the ability of individuals and organizations to withstand and absorb breaches and failures rather than on a genuine collective effort to prevent them in the first place.

Such a path is not sustainable and owes much to the "customer" prism of organizing and viewing online activity. The commonality enjoining individuals and organizations in the market realm is an implicit or explicit trade-off between convenience and privacy (a central premise of the digital wallet). By allowing one's personal information to be readily shared across interested parties, the potential increases to have more tailored product and service offerings along with more integrated and innovative forms of transaction bundling. Thus, a reputable online retailer will gather and analyze individual purchasing patterns and make recommendations accordingly (a common practice by Amazon to note just one widely used example), with data sets from such transacting routinely shared and sold with other market entities (a sharing largely facilitated by the terms of consent agreements that most consumers blindly embrace upon completing an online transaction of one sort or another).

Social networking can thus be seen as an enjoining of commerce and community in a manner that further subsumes privacy as an individual cost (in terms of limiting gains from convenience and connection) rather than a collective investment for society as a whole. While many join social networks oblivious to any commercial considerations, looking instead for connections to existing and new communities of friends, family, colleagues, and acquaintances, the dynamics of convenience stemming from tailored and innovative market offerings themselves derived from massive data mining efforts is a critical driver of infrastructure development and expansion by the companies housing social media activity and seeking profitability in doing so. The future of Facebook is thus said to be inextricably linked to its ability to generate revenues from mobile advertising, underscoring the friction between individualized privacy and protection and the widening fusion of community and commerce.

Due to the aforementioned establishment of Privacy Commissioners and like-minded guardians of privacy rights, social media sites such as Facebook and Twitter have become more transparent and genuine in their offering of tools and choices to users to augment their own privacy safeguards while also facing more stringed government reporting and oversight in response to widening examples of misuse and breaches of user trust.[10] Yet this market-laden logic of choice, underpinned by the commercialized nature of the infrastructure itself, may further weaken any collective ethos of responsibility and selfgovernance by users (indeed the public sector may also accentuate this danger as public servants and elected officials gravitate to such sites and trumpet the benefits of 'joining the conversation').

This latter point is central since social media sites and cloud-enabled virtualization permeate widening and deepening facets of societal and political activity (much as Facebook presents itself as a social utility), engraining such infrastructures into the behavioral ethos of the collective governance of a jurisdiction as a whole. While Facebook Google, and other technology giants clearly have a strong interest in safeguarding the security of their infrastructures and the overall resilience of the Internet—to the extent they can (and they are considerably aided by open source dynamics that augment their collective capacity for doing so), it is not in their mission or mandate to directly foster offsetting civic and collective capacities for personal responsibility and self-governance that could erode their capacities for synergistic information sharing and openness that drive their profitability.

The necessity of more active forms of public awareness, vigilance, and involvement (and by extension the escalating risks of passive acceptance and ignorance) can only augment going forward, in what Wolf describes as the "data-driven life" emerging from the interplay of four fundamental alterations to the relationship between people, data, and technology:

> First, electronic sensors got smaller and better. Second, people started carrying powerful computing devices, typically disguised as mobile phones. Third, social media made it normal to share everything. And fourth, we begin to get an inkling of the rise of a global super-intelligence known as the cloud. (p. 11, Young 2012)

As Young points out, current approaches to managing data are poorly suited to this new environment: are "the systems we have in place around contracts and consent and rights are really designed for an analog era, an older informational ecosystem" (p. 183, ibid.). Part of her proposed basis for new solutions and a preservation

---

[10] In August 2012 Facebook and the US Government announced a settlement pertaining to the company's privacy policies and practices—featuring two decades of government-led audits and a commitment by the company to garner explicit approval from users before any subsequent changes to what sort of information on the social media site is made available publicly or otherwise shared.

of the digital self in an increasingly virtual and by extension data-driven environment is an emphasis on the value and importance of personal responsibility. She thus calls upon individuals to become "data activists" in moving beyond passive usage and acceptance of new informational offerings that bundle, share, and integrate data in incomprehensible and seemingly opaque manners—and to seek greater openness, understanding, and vigilance in determining appropriate privacy-trade-offs both individually and collectively.

Such a reorientation of privacy as much about responsibility as rights provides an encouraging middle ground between the extremities of those seeking privacy guarantees and those instead viewing privacy as unrealistic or simply out of date. It can also draw sustenance from the collective and distributed dynamics of open-source communities that have sought some degree of balance between open collaboration and competition in fostering new innovations in both back-end infrastructure and content creation.

There is an important relationship here to a central message of the preceding chapter—namely, that the increasingly porous and complex cybersecurity challenges facing governments and entire jurisdictions require governance innovation beyond the traditional bureaucratic prism of public sector action and accountability. In a similar vein, categorical and starkly codified approaches to treating privacy as an enshrined right (and often an entitlement of a widening cadre of online activity) mask the wider complexities and set of interdependencies at play. A combination of cloud-based infrastructures and mobile devices coupled with networks of public and private sector organizations sharing and processing information render simplistic assurances a dangerously misleading fallacy, an important lesson of Young's portrayal and assessment of a data-driven life (Young 2012).

Yet with respect to the role and direct functioning and contributions of public sector authorities—both administrative and political—a key challenge in this regard lies in the fact that the advent of e-government over the past two decades has largely taken place in a manner that has embraced the customer mindset and sought to apply it widely to state reforms and strategies (Dutil et al. 2010). Moreover, the fragmented and commercialized behavior of democratic agents online (notably political parties), first noted in this book's introduction and returned to prominently in the next chapter, further reinforce individualization and rights at the expense of collective obligation and responsibilities.

By contrast, calls for heightened engagement and vigilance with respect to privacy and security can only find resonance in a political environment conducive for such an orientation (i.e., one where citizens are empowered with not only rights and protections but also tools for self-empowerment as well as collective awareness and dialogue). In other words, the commercial must be complemented with the political—better balancing and aligning rights and responsibilities as individuals execute roles as both consumers and citizens.

With respect to these latter, citizen-centered and more collective perspectives, the evolution of more digital and mobile democratic processes becomes central to orchestrating such a cultural realignment and rebalancing. Consistent with a key lesson of the previous chapter, public engagement and collective learning are central to crafting both personal and organizational strategies for proactive awareness and self-responsibility—and appropriate measures for institutional adaptation for a jurisdiction as whole. Democratic and public engagement and the mixed prospects for such forms of participation are thus the focus of the next chapter.

Chapter 7
Deliberation and Engagement

E-Democracy in Many Forms

In parallel to more open and participative governance movements associated with mobility, there has been a widening interest in linking the Internet with new forms of democracy—what some have termed as the search for "legitimacy 2.0" (Mindus et al. 2011). Underpinned by the wider canvas of the democratization of information across societies discussed throughout this book, proponents of reform and critics of the status quo have thus sought to foster an alternative paradigm less rooted in historical foundations and increments of change and more aligned with more virtual realities. The following quote is indicative of this desire to chart a new path:

> An online democracy cannot and should not mirror the procedures of traditional democratic institutions, but must instead be designed to reflect the fundamental requirements of democracy (consent, legitimacy) in a form that is suited to the unique conditions and human behaviour of the Internet. (p. 71, Fatland 2007)

Within existing political institutions, the emergence of aspirations for some form of online participation and engagement has been steady in formation and ascent over the past decade. For instance, whereas the United Nations Global E-government Survey in 2003 found that "Only very few governments have opted to use e-government applications for transactional services or for networking...Even fewer governments use it to support the genuine participation of citizens in politics," subsequent reviews in 2010 and 2012 would catalogue and rank widening experimentation in this regard. Similarly, a 2011 report on "The Future of Government" by the World Economic Forum calls for flatter and more innovative forms of democratic governance featuring online processes for citizen engagement (World Economic Forum 2011).

Despite such sentiment and growing unity on the need for more participation, the examples above illustrate the difficulties that can ensue due to both the inertia of traditional representational models and the diversity of viewpoints as to what should either accompany or ultimately replace them (Macintosh 2003; Roy 2006, 2008,

J. Roy, *From Machinery to Mobility: Government and Democracy in a Participative Age*, 83
Public Administration and Information Technology 2, DOI 10.1007/978-1-4614-7221-6_7,
© Springer Science+Business Media New York 2013

2012c; Reddick and Aikins 2012). While participatory perspectives on democratic reform predate the Internet and the e-government era, they have been significantly strengthened due to the online potentials for sharing information and mobilizing collective action—although as discussed early on in this book, the Internet has also reinforced the abilities of governments to control information and assert their power in more centralized manners. Accordingly, numerous design tensions present themselves, albeit underpinned by a widening canvas of perspectives illuminating the potential and the need for more direct and discursive capacities of democratic engagement (Shane 2004; Wyld 2007; Shirky 2008; McNutt 2009).

Building on work undertaken by the OECD, Macintosh, and others, three levels of online involvement reflect an evolution from essentially becoming better informed on issues to becoming engaged in dialogue and debate to ultimately becoming empowered to exert influence:

> E-enabling, which encompasses accessibility and understanding (information);
> E-engaging, which requires consulting a wider audience to enable deeper contributions and support deliberative debate on policy issues (consultation); and
> E-empowering, providing opportunities for citizens to influence and participate in policy formulation and service design (participation). (p. 2, Sommer and Cullen 2009)

Importantly, as these definitions imply, the second and third levels of online involvement require something of a virtuous cycle between deliberation and participation.[1] Fueled by the widening capacities for spontaneous and grassroots mobilization (of the sort underpinning Shirky's fluid and organic notions of governance first reviewed in Chap. 2, any evolution from enabling to engagement and empowerment nonetheless faces stiff head winds stemming from tensions between machinery and mobility. At the core of such tensions in terms of democratic processes is the challenge of deliberation.

The Deliberative Challenge

Since the advent of the Internet, electronic democracy (e-democracy) has brought many meanings and potentials. At a basic level, it can mean an incremental layering over existing processes—such as leveraging the Internet for online voting or instead an additional channel of informing the public both during and between elections. Both such examples reflect an application of the Internet to existing or incrementally evolving models of representational democracy. At the same time, however, and in a manner analogous to technology's evolution and tensions between proprietary and open-source design, the Internet has also contributed to a more democratized society—that in turn fuels pressure on formal democratic institutions to not only retool but to face fundamental renewal and reinvention.

---

[1] Indeed, going forward in this book, we will not distinguish between engagement and empowerment, viewing the space in between these two levels as the essence of "participation and engagement" as discussed and titled in this chapter.

One academic symposium sponsored by the European Commission, for example, summarized the contours of this debate in terms of the following five questions: what type of democracy do we want, what values do we want e-democracy to emphasize, how do individual devices affect behavior (citizens, politicians, and other stakeholders), how can individual devices link to policy decisions and outcomes, and what criteria should we use for evaluating democracy and how can evaluations help democratic development (p. 63, Kotsiopoulos 2009)? The report further observes with respect to the first question that "While it is not the role of any individual to decide how democracy should work in a particular country, governments and others need to reflect upon how democracy currently works and what problems they really want to address" (ibid.).

Recent financial crises globally coupled with the resilience of traditional democratic culture have arguably diminished the urgency of democratic reform in favor of economic priorities (a matter further explored in the next chapter). Yet considerable evidence also suggests widening public disenchantment with such an approach—and a growing appetite for alternative democratic methodologies predicated on enhanced consultative and participative capacities (Shane 2004; Kettl 2005; Reddick and Aikins 2012; Lacigova et al. 2012). Resolving such tensions and facilitating collective reflection as to the form and workings of democracy begins with the central notion of deliberation (Shane 2004; Fatland 2007; Kingwell 2010).

Within representational models of democracy, deliberation and debate have traditionally been housed within legislative chambers such as Parliaments and Congress. As discussed in Chap. 2, concentrating power at the apex of the executive branch is a trend predating the Internet but also deepened by it as Prime Ministers, Premiers, and Presidents have become the all-encompassing faces of their governments. In response to the resulting centralizing tendencies internally and a more informed citizenry and increasingly diverse and aggressive media environment externally, exchanges within legislatures have often become more theatrical than substantive, subsumed by a wider policy-making and policy arena much more diffused and dispersed than the shielded and codified confines of legislative chambers.

Greater public awareness, however, does not naturally generate informed and structured deliberation of the sort sought within the limited confines of legislative chambers designed for such a purpose. For many observers, greater accessibility to opinions and platforms to express one's opinions (individually and in concert with like-minded partisans and commentators) accentuates divides and distrust. Deliberation thus breaks down, replaced by what Kingwell terms "the shout doctrine"—a deterioration of democracy driven by an inverse relationship between transparency and civility:

> But relatively little attention has been given to discursive versions of collective action problems, perhaps because we naively assume that transparency will govern political exchanges; we think we know what the other person's interests and actions are. This assumption is false. Discourse, no less than consumption, has positional and hence competitive aspects. Indeed, winning the argument — or, rather, being seen to win it — is the essence of many discursive exchanges, especially political ones. If politics is reduced to elections or debates, it goes from being a shared undertaking of articulating ends and means and becomes a game of status and one-upmanship. (p. 2, Kingwell 2010)

An alternative and more inherently optimistic portrait of democracy's present evolution would begin with the viewpoint that such exchanges reflect a freedom of information and expression that are core to democracy—and thus a heightened form of societal collective intelligence to underpin political debate and any eventual action. Nevertheless, the central problem with this view is that such unstructured exchange can often be both opaque and sharply divisive across what becomes a more fragmented and polarized citizenry. Conditions for collective learning and deliberative compromise diminish accordingly.

Commercializing and Utilitarian Tendencies

In further dissecting the deliberative challenge, it is important to consider the ethical underpinnings of individual values that shape behavior and decision-making. Two competing schools of thought offer an important contrast in this regard: (1) deontological ethics, focusing on the nature and moral grounding of the decision itself, and (2) teleological ethics, examining consequences and outcomes (Hull 1979; Kernaghan and Langford 1990; Roy 2012c). The former, rooted in the theoretical underpinnings of Kantian moral imperatives, asks what essentially renders a decision to be inherently good; it is process-driven in terms of respecting basic precepts irrespective of the outcomes of doing so. Conversely, the latter builds upon a more calculating and rational viewpoint of the individual concerned first and foremost with his or her own welfare—and as such it is often termed as utilitarian in reflecting the theorizing of Bentham and others who have been so important in shaping modern economic theory (ibid.).

The key distinction here lies between an inherent respect for and upholding of rules (beyond codified laws to also include more implicit and shared principles and customs) versus implicit and explicit determinations of net benefit—and therefore weighing the risks and costs of various courses of action. Whereas deontology is thus more suited to responsibilities and duties of citizenship that have underpinned what has traditionally been termed as a "social contract" with the state, teleological perspectives of public behavior are guided by a more individualistic and competitive calculus of self-interest as well as right-oriented protections and privileges afforded by public sector resources and actions.

With respect to the evolution of online governance, there is much evidence to suggest that within existing institutional structures, the emphasis by governments themselves has most predominantly been on the commercial-teleological perspectives of virtual interactions between state actors and the public at large (Dutil et al. 2010; Roy 2012c). Citizens, for example, are increasingly referred to as customers—and in many jurisdictions, governments themselves have prioritized a service-centric view of e-government that implicitly or otherwise embraces comparisons between online industry and marketplace dynamics and those in the public sector realm (ibid.). Whereas governments exert their guardian duties emphasizing deontological underpinnings in many key areas such as privacy, for example (with varying viewpoints as to their effectiveness in doing so), what is far less prevalent online, again consistent with the argumentation of the preceding chapter, is a language of duty and obligations on the part of the citizenry.

Two key questions thus arise in terms of democracy and its deliberative conduct:

- First, whether or not an online ethos that seems increasingly teleological and commercial in orientation can facilitate new forms of inclusive and collective action as a basis for updated mechanisms of learning and compromise that previously took place within formal legislative chambers (populated with elected officials acting on behalf of constituents far less informed and educated than is the case today)
- Secondly, can mobility and social media foster dialogue and more participative democratic governance models that lessen and ultimately bridge the widening divide between a more informed public seeking new opportunities for engagement and existing structures of representational democracy (no longer functioning as initially designed)?

In a manner akin to the previous chapter's assertion of the need for a culture of wider responsibility to underpin both individual and collective security, the answer to the first question is—in my estimation—clearly no.

Evidence to date from Canada and elsewhere suggests an enlargement and relative imposition of a more commercial orientation that emphasizes values such as competition, efficiency, and convenience—and a more teleological approach to decision-making based upon a rational weighing of interests, outcomes, and consequences (Dutil et al. 2010). Aside from explaining much of the current political disenchantment on display in many democracies at present, such a viewpoint stems from much of the argumentation in this book and also finds a widening cadre of related viewpoints such as Nabatchi's persuasive case for a "citizenship deficit" increasingly handicapping trust and legitimacy (Nabatchi 2010).

Addressing and rectifying such a deficit requires both deontological and discursive elements to give rise to a set of conditions conducive to genuine forms of democratic engagement. By engagement, we refer to elevated levels of public involvement that emphasize power-sharing between decision-makers and the public and corresponding mechanisms to facilitate such involvement in ways that carry recognizable and measurable linkages between participation and outcomes.[2] Whereas e-government has largely come to be defined by online service apparatuses primarily teleological in orientation and function, a bolstered deontological dimension to online governance in the public sector realm would necessitate an expansion of legislative and political processes to overlap with and make use of new forms of social media—along with strategies to shape the sorts of participation occurring in new social media and how meaningful conversation and collective learning can ensue. A widening cadre of online tools and platforms at the very

---

[2] Such a definition is in keeping with and largely stems from the "spectrum of public participation" created by the International Association for Public Participation:
http://iap2.org/associations/4748/files/Spectrum.pdf

least make obligatory forms of engagement potentially feasible (Roy 2011; Williamson 2011; Reddick and Aikins 2012).

The major challenge that must be recognized, addressed, and overcome is the predominant and pervasive emphasis on rights and choice which—by design or unwittingly (depending in part on motives and ideology)—subsumes democracy within an individualizing and largely utilitarian ethos of choice and commercialization. While it is true that both commercial and civil society endeavors share a voluntary aspect (more based upon self-interest and private gain in the former versus collective and shared interests in the latter), the state's distinguishing attribute has historically comprised important elements of duties and responsibilities all too often diminished in the Internet era.

A requirement to engagement also implies opportunities and venues to do so—beyond the shackles of today's partisan and media cleavages that facilitate messaging and competition at the expense of collaborative and reasoned deliberation (Samara 2010; Roy 2011). Accordingly, new mechanisms for political involvement must be forged, and such mechanisms must include online channels and forums that (1) significantly bolster the online presence and purpose of legislative branches of government, (2) facilitate new and wider deliberative capacities between elected officials and the citizenry (enjoining them in new ways), and (3) emphasize both the duties and benefits of political awareness and engagement (Public Policy Forum 2012). Analogous to the demographic-driven viewpoints on workforce and managerial transformation presented in earlier chapters of this book, such changes are particularly important to younger segments of the citizenry less observant of deferential authority and structure and more ideologically pluralistic and varied than traditional partisan formation and identities (ibid.).

Political parties are central to such debate. In a thoughtful analysis examining their future, Rogers concludes that "the era of the mass parties is almost certainly over" (p. 609, Rogers 2005). In line with the view that (1) people are increasingly political but less partisan and (2) parties in their present form are being reduced to fund-raising and spin-driven marketing operations, his conclusion is that new and more varied forms of political movements are required, quite possibly in formation only after the election of legislators that would ideally reflect more grassroots and interactive relations with constituents. In line with the governance trends and tensions first discussed in Chap. 2, a less rigid and partisan and more participatory ethos requires institutional alterations to foster innovative forms of involvement freed from today's engrained notions of partisan identity and organization.[3]

---

[3] As discussed further below, such a basis for more direct and less partisan involvement already exists in many jurisdictions at the local level—where not coincidentally governments are leading in the embracement of digital experimentation aimed at wider and more direct and collaborative forms of citizen engagement with both appointed and elected officials. Although the local scene is far from a nirvana of democratic renewal, and while its structuring and conduct is shaped by national institutions and cultures, it nonetheless provides a more feasible laboratory and window upon current incremental changes that may yield more insight into prospects and conditions for more widespread change and reform as democracies and public administration adapts more fully to a still-nascent mobility era.

Seeking a more deliberative flavor to such new forms of involvement requires a theoretical vantage point separate from the aforementioned deontological and teleological schools of thought. Consistent with the advent of Web 2.0 and the basis of open and collaborative governance first sketched out in Chap. 2, democratic theorists have often turned to Habermas for inspiration here—and the central importance of the conditions for structuring and nurturing conversation. Linking conversations to discourse, Orr explains:

> Definitions of deliberation focus on distinguishing it from other forms of speech. As Simone Chambers points out in her outline of Habermas's discourse and democratic practices, "not just any conversation is a discourse". Conversations are only discursive if they approximate the ideal conditions of discourse (Chambers 1995: 234). It is only through true deliberation that the purpose of the public sphere becomes obvious. The ability for citizens to discuss public matters with each other is an essential ingredient for developing public opinion and fostering civic engagement. (Zhou et al. 2008: 761) (p. 9, Orr 2010)

Dahlgren links this ability of citizens to discuss matters with their willingness to do so via what he articulates as civic cultures, a basis for deepening the deliberative dimensions of a more online public sphere (Dahlgren 2005). The prospects for doing so would seem decidedly mixed. On the one hand, the aforementioned argumentation of excessive partisanship and an interrelated commercializing ethos (teleological leaning in terms of behavioral values) suggests a world poorly suited to a deepened civic dimension (and one, in contrast, more prone to Kingwell's shout doctrine). On the other hand, the widening participatory nature of the Internet's Web 2.0 platforms and methodologies features self-organizing associations and movements driving virtual and more collaborative governance models that suggest a potential for deploying them toward more explicitly civic-minded undertakings.

Traditional and New Media

With respect to the second question above—specifically pertaining to the potential for discursive dimensions of social media usage and deployment—a deeper consideration of the role of media as a gatekeeper and a mechanism for both gathering and making use of information in a fluid technological setting is required. Indeed, in shaping an online ethos, the media has a tremendously important role to play—though in understanding this role and how it is changing, we must distinguish between the "traditional media" versus the so-called new or social media. Whereas the former is predicated upon professionalized intermediaries and a passive public receiving filtered and prepared content, the latter is user-driven and much more spontaneous and networked in terms of both content creation and its consumption and sharing.

Prior to the Internet, a robust debate existed between the relative size and influence of public versus private media—as the former was said to provide an important platform for matters and discussions more oriented to the public interest (and guardian functions). In many jurisdictions, the media has been referred to as a fourth branch of government, exercising oversight capacities on behalf of citizens, a responsibility in most democracies shared between publicly and privately owned entities nonetheless bound by a common journalistic ethos comprising at the very least a healthy mix of both deontological and teleological values sets.

Such a journalistic ethos partly underpinned the functioning and stability of representational democracy in two important ways: firstly, professional journalists have acted as key intermediaries between politicians and political processes and the public at large, and secondly, journalists and politicians themselves colluded either formally or discreetly and indirectly in determining the relative boundaries between public and private spaces in the affairs and lives of those elected to office. This latter, uneasy balancing act thus reinforced the secretive cultural orientation of most democratic models—as journalists sought to accept some basic limitations on their reporting in exchange for regular access and civil and productive relations with governing authorities (a compact nonetheless circumvented in times of extreme or sensational acts deemed in the public interest by journalistic organizations—balancing their own set of commercial and deontological incentives in doing so).

As today's digital environment has dramatically altered the contours of media presence and ownership, the ethos of media coverage and behavior has altered in important ways. The Internet's empowerment of new and more direct forms of citizen journalism—as well as more militant whistle-blowing formations such as WikiLeaks—has occurred within a widening imposition of a nexus between commercialization and sensationalism. A more informed public ensues, but one more oriented toward roles as consumers of constant news flows rather than enlightened and deliberative citizens. In a 2012 address to graduates at the University of Massachusetts (Amherst), a prominent television American journalist offered this portrait of new media's evolution and the dangers arising:

> Even over the relatively brief span of my life-time, I have seen the telephone evolve technologically from a rotary dial system, on which long-distance phone calls had to be placed through an operator, to this—(HOLD UP Iphone). (I am not, as you might imagine, big on Apps.) Still, I get it. You cannot spend a lifetime in radio and television, and not appreciate the value of instant, near-universal communication.
>
> But it is both the blessing and curse of our time that media have never been equipped for greater speed and universal reach than now. Speed, you see, is often the enemy of accuracy and clarity… Political debate is a wonderful thing; but partisan shrieking is corrosive and destructive. If we are to find solutions to the challenges we face, we have to re-learn the virtues of compromise.
>
> If we are going to deal intelligently with the problems we confront, we need time to pause, to consider and reflect. But our media, news and social, are intolerant of anything but an instant response. We are making and receiving endless observations about the trivial, and believe that we are communicating. I am left with a feeling of not just great opportunities missed, but with a sense of actual danger to our republic.[4]

---

[4]Source: *Twitter is not a typewriter*: Ted Koppel's Commencement Address at UMass Amherst (http://stearns.wordpress.com/2012/05/14/twitter-is-not-a-typewriter-ted-koppels-commencement-address-at-umass-amherst/)

Much of this concern stems from and is fuelled by the rise of mobile devices and social media but also how these new forums impact and shape traditional media outlets and patterns. Traditional media outlets—notably television journalistic programming devoted to political affairs, for example—have sought to augment their own participatory linkages with their audiences via tools such as online polls and constant Twitter feeds on the screen to accompany more traditional forms of on-screen reporting and debate. Accordingly, viewers are invited to "join the conversation" although the primary incentives and impacts to do so are most often self-promotion, provocation, and entertainment: real-time viewer polls are similarly reductionist, and while a form of connection and expression, it is naive and arguably dangerous to characterize such actions as conversational.

The resulting conditions perpetuate Kingwell's "shout doctrine" as viewpoints and opinions are reinforced and engrained rather than refined through open and reasoned exchanges and dialogue, underpinning Koppel's pessimistic portrayal of online media sketched out above and leading to a sense that despite widening experimentation by governments themselves, capacities for collective and discursive engagement remain underdeveloped (Pole 2011; Reddick and Aikins 2012).

Toward Open-Source Democracy

The advent of open-source design principles—underpinning the emergence of cloud computing and social media as the back-end and frontend dimensions to both technological mobility and social and organizational participation, all inherently democratic in scope—has ironically made only modest strides in recasting formal political architectures of even self-described democracies (where, for reasons discussed, countervailing forces against wider and novel democratization are equally on display). Furthering efforts to strengthen deliberative and civic-minded capacities are dependent upon finding ways to successfully leverage wider and more networked forms of collective intelligence in ways that rebalance virtual and physical channels and interactions in accordance with the spreading of online life on the one hand and the heightened (if as yet untapped) potential for participative and deliberative democracy on the other hand.

Building on a dissection of open-source dynamics within the software design community, Shirky highlights the specific tipping point of modification and improvement occurring online as one otherwise isolated designer essentially crowd-sources a particular dilemma to an open, unstructured, and potentially collaborative community of expertise and solution providers enjoined by shared identities and objectives. In a similar vein, Kostakis presents the foundations of how such openness and participation can apply to the democratization, in a more direct and participative sense, of the formal political sphere:

> "Open source democracy" (a concept introduced by Rushkoff 2003) is related to a "model for the open-ended and participatory process through which legislation might occur in a networked democracy" (p. 56). Members of open source communities experience the way that their actions affect the whole and, as a result, they are more conscious of "how their

moment-to-moment decisions can be better aligned with the larger issues with which they are
concerned" (Rushkoff 2003, pp. 60–61)….In a nutshell, it tries to redefine modern democratic
discourse in the digital information age. Open source activity is, in some ways, similar to
"crowdsourcing," although I prefer using the term open source because it stresses concepts
such as openness, the common good, and collaboration. (p. 12, Kostakis 2011)

Based upon his examination of an application of such a philosophy to three specific models of participatory democracy—including models both within and outside
of the formal confines democracy and government—the author finds significant
potential and measurable progress toward open deliberation and shared innovation
as a basis for addressing complexity in less conventional and more collaborative
ways. To once again quote Kostakis,

The investigation of the three cases of wikipolitics (Deliberatorium, wikipolitics.gr, and
Future Melbourne) showed that their empirical results so far seem positive and capable of
splitting the traditional hierarchical paradigm. In general, all the examined cases showed
that there are possibilities for large numbers of people to effectively collaborate in the formulation and the evaluation of a wide range of ideas regarding the solution of complex
problems. (p. 25, ibid.)

Despite such potential, the author strikes a more cautious tone in terms of the
collective ability of societies to reinvent formal political institutions and processes
in accordance with open-source principles and methodologies—as a host of potential barriers and pitfalls present themselves (ibid.). Nevertheless, in light of the fact
that we are approximately 20 years into the mainstream adoption of virtual platforms and online tools—in comparison to several centuries of evolving practices of
traditional representational mindsets and mechanisms—the path ahead seems clear
with respect to societal expectations and behavior even as it shall remain a significantly contested endeavor.

A corresponding political culture inherently more supportive of the leveraging
of collective intelligence through more discursive and collaborative approaches
than presently allowable within representational architectures thus requires not
only a new language (the basis of which is seemingly identifiable) but also a shared
capacity to embrace and deploy this new language toward common purpose. As
Williamson rightly underlines, "The internet does not of itself change an individual's motivation to become engaged, what it does do is reduce the barriers to engagement and hence lowers the motivational threshold at which citizens choose to
engage" (p. 26, 2011). The author thus presents what he defines as an "emergent
e-democracy lifecycle encompassing six evolutionary stages: entrenched positions, building awareness, disruption to existing processes, new ways to engage,
shift in balance in power, and perceived value (ibid.)".

This cycle would apply well to the evolution of open-source software and its
upending of traditional proprietary models of innovation and ownership. Moreover,
it carries equal resonance for an optimistic and constructive project of democratic
adaptation and renewal (since as the discussions and examples of this book illustrate, we remain somewhere midway through this cycle—depending on jurisdiction
and experimentation, with at the very least a widening potential to move toward the
latter stages). A review of some current experimentation with social media engagement underscores this point and further illuminates the challenges at hand.

Social Media and Bottom-Up Engagement

Prodded by a more informed, online, and participative society, governments have begun to recognize the challenges described above and respond accordingly. For instance, the City of New York has attempted to articulate how social media is an enabler of both enhanced service and public engagement: the digital city "road map" includes four interrelated dimensions—open government, access, industry, and engagement (New York City 2011). Related research of US municipalities demonstrates a widening set of experiments underway by local authorities to link social media usage with engagement-oriented purposes and objectives (Mossberger and Wu 2012). The key distinction here lies in moving beyond a traditional communication mindset and not only to seek input and feedback in a consultative manner but to link such participation to decisions and outcomes via "good conversations":

> Of course the public should play a central role in deciding what represents value for money in public services, but the current approach is unlikely to foster any meaningful deliberation or empowerment. What we need more of is public debate, or "good conversations" between professionals and communities to avoid officials losing touch in the first place. The appropriate place to achieve this is local government because circumstances vary in different parts of the country. (p. 4, Viitanen 2010)

This quote thus incites a reflection as to which level of government is best placed to lead participative engagement via social media—since national level entities often have greater fiscal resources and digital visibility, whereas local authorities benefit from closer proximity to community constituents and are better able to blend online and off-line processes. Indeed, emphasizing these localized advantages, Carr-West (2009) outlines a basis for proceeding with social media through localized models of experimentation and collaborative and open innovation involving four directions:

> Free people to innovate: allow council staff and community members to be driven by their passions. Online engagement tools don't require massive IT infrastructures or budgets, they can be pulled together from free web tools. If people want to build something, let them.
>
> Try everything: it's no good waiting for the perfect tool. We're in an era of restless technological change and if you try and work out exactly how to match tools to the job, the tools (and possibly the job) will have changed before you even get started.
>
> Be open about what you're doing: particularly where it is experimental and be clear about what worked and what didn't.
>
> Allow good ideas to emerge: wherever they come from and however much they disrupt established hierarchies or ways of working. (p. 8, Carr-West 2009)

The emergence of "open data" initiatives—examined in the fourth chapter—reflects elements of shared ownership models and openness with respect to information as less a proprietary and strategic asset than a public resource and social utility. Driven by the rise of social media and collective intelligence on the one hand and the emphasis in recent years on citizen engagement and participatory democracy on the other hand, such strategies are at their core about leveraging social media as a platform for wider public involvement and deliberation. While the design of apps is arguably a more individualized process, their adaptation and wider usage within the community promotes and indeed requires collaborative and discursive elements.

In Canada, as examples of this bottom-up emergence of alternatives, one can point to Mayor Nenshi of Calgary—a strong proponent of social media usage for both electoral and community engagement purposes—and the City of Edmonton for its pioneering efforts in open data and a community "app" competition underpinned by a municipal infrastructure increasingly gravitating to cloud systems and mobility-inspired governance principles. Such examples are consistent with research underscoring that electronic and online democracy has taken hold much more quickly and in more participatory manners at subnational as opposed to national levels (Shane 2004; Sloam 2007; Mossberger and Wu 2012).

The City of Toronto, by contrast, has displayed some of the uniqueness of local democracy—and its absence of formal political parties which lessens the potential for a concentration of power by single leaders. Despite the media-driven visibility of Mayor Rob Ford (whose election was attributed to a strong usage of one-way social media efforts in messaging and fund-raising), many of his plans have been thwarted or altered by the relative messiness of a local Council comprised of individually elected members—themselves representing a much more diverse set of social media and online practices.[5]

Indeed, across the Province of Ontario, nearly one-half of all municipal governments had embraced some form of social media usage by 2012 (primarily Facebook and Twitter), an increase of nearly 700 % in a mere 2 years (Timoshenko and Demers 2012). The City of Guelph's formally adopted social media guidelines are indicative of a localized movement for wider engagement (in keeping with the above assertions of Carr-West) as their five principles begin the importance of listening while emphasizing ongoing ties and collective participation:

> i) Listen—listen to what people are saying before joining the conversation; ii) Engage—invite ideas and encourage discussion (Social media is rooted in conversations, relationships, exchanges, shared ideas, and common interests); iii) Enable—enable people to share your content with their own networks (herein lies the power of social media); iv) Share—be friendly, and be honest, share your expertise with your audience (the more you do the more likely you are to foster meaningful relationships); and v) Participate—post regularly and be prepared to engage people.[6]

This emergence of more consultative and participative forms of deploying social media by local authorities is a small but significant step toward adapting democratic engagement to the age of mobility. Consistent with the notion of public value management first introduced in Chap. 2, a more open and deliberative prism of governance places participation and engagement at the heart of such an evolution—requiring that "requires that public managers cultivate new forms of dialogue, deliberation,

---

[5] See, for example, the Toronto City Council Social Media Report Card as one compilation of such practices by elected officials: http://campaignimpossible.blogspot.ca/

[6] Summarized from the following source, a research consultancy having gathered such policies and guidelines from numerous municipalities across the Province and elsewhere: http://www.redbrick.ca/assets/file/resource/City-of-Guelph---Social-Media---Guiding-Principles-for-City-Spokespeople.pdf

and relationship with citizen stakeholders" (Stoker 2005; Dutil et al. 2010; Lips 2012; Reddick and Aikins 2012).

With respect to open data strategies, similarly, an early and recent examination of Canadian government efforts, federally and provincially, complements this perspective by framing the "holy grail" question of open data strategies as if and the extent to which data is being used by citizens to generate value in any direct or indirect manner (Helbig et al. 2012). Whereas a rubric of traditional public administration would likely emphasize instead the costs of gathering and making available such data, new public management would envision determinations of value through a more economically driven calculation of net benefits in a largely identifiable and thus quantifiable manner. Public value management, by contrast, seeks to recognize the synergistic effects of deliberative networks and upfront engagement leading not only to altered government actions and initiatives but also to those originating from within the community at large. While an "app" competition is a specific example of such externalized contributions, the participative nexus between information openness and deliberative engagement carries much wider ramifications for strengthening collective intelligence, learning, and adaptive-based governance—and thus the reforming of traditional representative democratic institutions and their functioning.

From the point of view of the public sector, then, the widening and deepening of technological mobility and the like-minded pursuit of collective intelligence must entail strategies, competencies, and capacities across three interrelated dimensions: information (and the shift to more transparent reporting and the provision of raw data in widely available and accessible manners), innovation (across policy and service processes encompassing both internal governance arrangements and those involving a more networked citizenry and set of partners and stakeholders), and intermediation (the set of mechanisms to facilitate ongoing deliberation and accountability via more active and collective engagement mechanisms).

Building upon the sorts of social media experimentations highlighted above, these interrelated dimensions call for a more fundamental refurbishment of public sector competencies and capacities than has been undertaken thus far. Some of the major elements identified from early experimentation include:

- The creation of a new organisational unit in order to organise and manage the presence of the government agency in these multiple eParticipation channels, and also to analyse the large quantities of both structured data (e.g. citizens' ratings) and unstructured data (e.g. citizens' postings in textual form) that will be created in these social media.
- Also, new processes should be established for the integration of the results and conclusions of the analysis of the above structured and unstructured eParticipation data in the decision and policymaking processes of government agencies.
- The human resources of these new units must have a particular culture (which is quite different culture from the dominant 'law enforcement' culture of government agencies) and specialised skills for managing efficiently the new electronic modes of communication. In general, government agencies should get accustomed to the style and language of interaction in the web 2.0 social media, and the whole culture around them, characteristics that are quite different compared with the official eParticipation spaces. (p. 87, Charalabidis et al. 2012)

Importantly, then, if more participative forms of digital and mobile democracy are to emerge within formal democratic institutions, it is locally where experimental innovations with altered roles and interrelationships between the public, politicians, and public servants are most likely to occur. Such a localized ethos is evident, for example, in Europe where researchers examining early case studies of social media usage and integration with online participation and formalized governance systems found significant potential for aligning off-line and virtual processes in ways that strengthen the overall engagement levels of the community (Mota and Santinha 2012). Realizing this potential entails an appropriate alignment between new media deployment, traditional public actors, and a genuinely engaged citizenry:

> The first point concerns the capacity of social media to transform virtual opinions and ideas into real initiatives.
>
> The second point is about the political reaction to civic movements that seek to counteract policy decisions designed without taking into consideration people's demands.
>
> The third point relates to the pedagogic and constructive nature of these civic movements and the way social media positively contribute to this purpose.
>
> The fourth and final point concerns the recognition of the social media technologies' significance in promoting citizens' joint effort to set direction for their community as a necessary but not sufficient condition for encouraging civic engagement and public participation in policy design and implementation. (p. 40, ibid.)

These four lessons underline the complex design challenges of social media as an engagement platform—rather than a mere extension of a government's communication apparatus (Mergel 2012a, b). They also underscore why it is locally where such innovation is most likely to occur, driven by a new generation of political leaders and civic activists more immersed in online behaviors and tools and thus more willing to envision and be open to new forms of more virtual and participative decision-making models.

Yet such localizing potential faces two significant sources of resistance, the first examined throughout this chapter—namely, an overriding commercialized and individualizing ethos of traditional media and much of online life and how such dynamics are unavoidably impacting democratic cultures and processes. In addition, the second source of resistance stems from the relative prominence of national politics and governance processes, often at the expense of their subnational counterparts. In an era of widening fiscal austerity, along with traditional structures of political federalism in many jurisdictions that reinforce national predominance, tensions between machinery and mobility are correspondingly intensified, an important dimension of public sector reform going forward and the focus of the final chapter.

Chapter 8
Austerity and Federalism

Money and Power

Perhaps nowhere is the cleavage between novel forms of democratic engagement—the focus of the preceding chapter—and the inertia of more entrenched and traditional practices greater than in the realm of fiscal planning and budgeting and the manner by which governments undertake and seek approval for their spending plans.

On the one hand, over the past decade there have been widening calls for more participative experimentation in budgeting exercises, and indeed many corresponding initiatives have resulted in tentative moves down such a path (Bertot et al. 2010a, b; Allegretti 2011). By contrast, with respect to the fundamental secrecy and top-down decision-making inherent to the Westminster model, governments have not strayed far from traditional practices, with the only significant degree of budgetary power-sharing determined by the relative majority or minority status of the governing party in the legislature.

In Australia, for instance, the budgets of Prime Minister Gillard's minority governments have been largely centralizing affairs—determined by the Prime Minster and her Minister of Finance, albeit further shaped by a limited set of negotiated trade-offs with a small number of independent and Green party allies to ensure Parliamentary passage. A similar set of eleventh hour, closed door negotiations would characterize Ontario, Canada's largest province, in 2012—a jurisdiction examined more closely below. In fairness, such are the workings of representational democracy, with many Westminster jurisdictions even going as far as formalizing the secrecy of the budget document up to the moment of its tabling. Elections and polls (and occasionally mass demonstrations) are often the limited means of influence and participation for the public. Elected officials and stakeholder representatives may, in turn, be consulted, but there is little in the way of genuine engagement.

J. Roy, *From Machinery to Mobility: Government and Democracy in a Participative Age*, 97
Public Administration and Information Technology 2, DOI 10.1007/978-1-4614-7221-6_8,
© Springer Science+Business Media New York 2013

Unfortunately, the checks and balances of the American Presidential model do not lead to a rosier portrait of citizen involvement. Despite President Obama's 2008 campaign pledges to foster more openness and collaboration—working across sharp partisan divides and with the public in new and more direct manners—any such aspirations were quickly stunted by a massive financial crisis (that in turn yielded—beginning under the final days of the Bush Administration—unprecedented secrecy and unilateralism in terms of bailout packages for financial institutions and the auto sector). Budgetary gridlock would ensure, for the entire first Obama mandate, the American Government functioning only due to periodic, short-term agreements with Congress, leading to the so-called fiscal cliff showdown as 2012 drew to a close (with ongoing conflict anticipated through 2013).

Within primarily representational models of democracy, a typical reaction to such paralysis is to seek greater clarity and centralization of authority—to seek a leader and a form of leadership to get things done. Such was the evolution of Barack Obama from a grassroots organizer and Washington outsider—promising a new form of politics—to Commander in Chief inheriting two wars and a massively destabilized national economy. President Obama's 2012 electoral victory would thus provide a strengthened hand in salvaging a year-end deal with a Republican-leaning Congress to raise taxes on the wealthiest Americans in order to avoid a wider set of tax increases for all taxpayers. Tellingly, a White House demand in late 2012 (immediately rejected by Congress) suggested shifting authority to raise the American debt ceiling from Congress to the President: the underlying dynamic at play to associate a crisis with gridlock and the need for more decisive and central-ized governance.

The centralization reflex can be seen in many US states as well—notably that of New York where Governor Cuomo has sought to reverse years of similar budgetary paralysis and other administrative scandals in an effort to stem rising public cyni-cism and public debt (and plummeting confidence in state institutions). Lauded by supporters for overcoming paralysis commonplace in past years, his unilateral lead-ership style has been characterized by many observers as highly centralist, arguably bringing the American governance model (albeit in this one particular jurisdiction[1]) closer to the workings of the Canadian Parliamentary model featuring, as discussed in Chap. 2, concentrated partisan authority and a penchant for information control. Indeed, under the auspices of a new Premier, the Provincial Government of Newfoundland would introduce reformed access to information legislation in June 2012 that was viewed by some informed critics as an affront to democratic account-ability (Alzner 2012).

This combination of economic and fiscal uncertainty and related and resulting ten-dencies toward more centralized decisiveness has similarly characterized Canadian

---

[1] Unlike President Obama, the Governor has been able to secure passage of his budgets via compromises with the legislature that have included structural changes to financial and oversight contracting practices that augment the direct purviews of the Governorship. See, for example, http://www.nytimes.com/2012/03/31/opinion/gov-cuomo-budgets-his-way.html

Prime Minister Harper: his first majority status budget in 2012 was thus framed as a much needed framework for economic growth and stability. The budget "omnibus" bill, however, proved widely controversial, sparking stalling tactics and an all-night marathon voting session (to no avail of course in light of the Government's majority in the legislature) due to the 452-page bill's inclusion of a wide array of reforms and initiatives only loosely associated with a literal interpretation of a budget (such an approach would nonetheless spark outrage and action by Aboriginal communities and their leaders, giving rise to the "Idle No More" protest movement[2]).

For Westminster traditionalists (typically including those politicians holding public office within such a system), there is little out of the ordinary here, notwithstanding long-standing concerns by outside observers pertaining to the concentration of power within the executive and offsetting erosion of the legislative branch (an erosion most pronounced in a Parliamentary setting with single party majority control). As first explained in Chap. 2, Canadian scholars and media commentators have exposed the main drivers and consequences of Prime Ministerial dominance. Some have also provided thoughtful reflections and recommendations aimed at reversing such a tide, including institutional alterations designed to both bolster legislative oversight and introduce new mechanisms for wider and novel forms of public engagement (McNutt 2009; Aucoin et al. 2011). However, within the context of majority-led government, the likelihood of such reforms being realized or even seriously explored is not high (the more IT-centric consequences of this majority mindset—generally and specific to Canada's Harper-led Conservative Government—are examined further below).

Beyond North America, more extreme versions of such schisms between democratization and centralization can be found in many parts of the world, notably in 2012 in both Mexico and Egypt.[3] Similar dynamics are also displayed in various European countries, such as Italy where austerity would lead, in 2011, to the temporary suspension of national democracy in favor of a technocrat and appointed Cabinet (albeit one that still requires Parliamentary approval to implement its spending reduction plans). Elected in 2012, French President Francois Hollande promised a more "normal Presidency" with wider and more meaningful power-sharing arrangements with Parliament and subnational government levels, only to see his party win an outright majority of seats in legislative elections, thereby cementing Presidential and Party authority across the National Assembly, the Senate, and most regions.

---

[2] With respect to Aboriginal affairs and the governance of the First Nations, the consequences of this absence of consultation (according to the First Nations) became visible for all to see in late 2012 and early 2013 with the "Idle No More" protest movement and the hunger strike of an Aboriginal Chief that would ultimately force the government into public meetings and promises of a new path going forward.

[3] A brief commentary, by this book's author, further elaborates on such examples (Democratic schisms: the clash of old and new voices): http://www.canadiangovernmentexecutive.ca/article/?nav_id=1014

The Ontario Premier Comes Full Circle

Prior to his Party's 2003 majority victory leading to his appointment as Premier of the Province of Ontario (an office he would occupy until early 2013[4]), Liberal leader Dalton McGuinty—in a manner not unlike the new French President—had promised to fundamentally alter democratic governance in the country's largest province (the population of which dwarfs many European nations). Accusing his predecessors of excessive secrecy and budgetary manipulation, McGuinty promised more financial transparency, one measure in a set of proposals for democratic renewal that would include electoral reform and the creation of "citizen's juries" as a means of more direct public involvement in policy-making.

Underpinning such proposals, the Internet was viewed as a key enabler of a positive cycle of transparency and trust and a corresponding refurbishment of democracy. When pressed by journalists, then-Opposition Leader McGuinty acknowledged that his proposals would significantly reduce the power of the Office of the Premier (due to more oversight and checks and balances on the otherwise unfettered authority of a majority Premier), a course he suggested that was necessary to breaking free from the shackles of centralized and secretive leadership that had become prevalent, in his view, over the preceding decade.

Having campaigned on a pledge to not increase taxes, once in power with a newly vested majority, the Premier almost immediately stunned the electorate with the introduction of a new health-care levy that was defended as tough and decisive leadership in order to salvage a crumbling and cherished public good. The move would encapsulate an approach to governing through successive majority years that deviated little from the steady trajectory of Westminster-based decision-making: at one point, the then-Premier himself publicly characterizing the art of governing as one of constant communications and campaign-mode-like messaging in order to proactively and reactively defend Government policy.

In 2011, the Premier would secure a third electoral victory, albeit in a manner just short of outright majority status and thus requiring support from the third party, New Democrats for legislative passage. Accordingly, in 2012 a crisis would ensue over the Government's budget and proposed modifications by the Opposition, leading to much public posturing and threats by the Premier to call an election in order to break the impasse. Underpinned by opinion polls suggesting little public appetite for another election, an 11th hour compromise would eventually enable approval of the budget—further illustrating the limited means of engagement on the part of the public on the one hand and a reversion to traditionalism on the part of the Ontario Premier on the other hand.

---

[4]The Premier announced his plans to retire in 2012—sparking a Party leadership contest and the January 2013 election of a new Leader, Kathleen Wynne, who was formerly sworn into the Premiership on February 11, 2013 (leading a minority government, as further explained below).

Reflecting tensions between machinery and mobility, the experiences of the now-former Premier of Ontario are indicative of the manner by which the Internet era can couple a more democratized society in terms of information flows and awareness and a more centralized polity. The latter stems from the traditions and evolution of a representational democratic model predicated more on stability and control than widened engagement, a dynamic arguably reinforced by economic uncertainty and pressures for fiscal austerity. A more extreme variant of this condition is displayed by the recent struggles of many European countries.

Europe's Post-democratic Age

In Europe, fiscal crises of various member states (notably, Greece, Italy, and Spain) have fuelled calls by many governments to further centralize various elements of financial and monetary governance at the European level (thereby deepening the administrative architecture of the European Union). For many observers, the risk of doing so is an accentuated cleavage between what might be termed European technocracy and its fledging and, as yet, very much underdeveloped democracy. Habermas describes what he views as Europe's post-democratic age: "a dangerous asymmetry has developed because to date the European Union has been sustained and monopolized only by political elites" (Habermas 2011). Though by no means the sole determinant, one important element of this asymmetry is the rise in complexity of European governance—and corresponding simplicity of austerity-driven solutions imposed upon various member countries (leading, in turn, to more polarized and extremist politics in many countries and even, as previously noted, a temporary suspension of democracy in Italy in order to oversee the imposition of austerity measures prescribed largely by European authorities and supranational bodies).

It should be acknowledged that Europe as a continental entity defies generalization, incubating as it does many robust jurisdictional examples both digitally and democratically (e.g., particularly in the north as observed in Chap. 6), along with the struggles of other member states and interrelated matters of wider European governance. The main point here is that the significant disconnect between the European populous and the political institutions of the European Union is analogous to the rising levels of cynicism and distrust accorded to national governments in the US and Canada. Moreover, as with the US debt crisis, ongoing fiscal and economic issues overshadow the sorts of efforts sought by Habermas and others to deepen citizenship and strengthen political culture. It is in this manner that Europe is arguably the world's most advanced laboratory of democratic diversity and experimentation with digital forms of engagement (with a strong local dimension to such experimentation as illustrated in the previous chapter), even as it struggles mightily with tensions between complexity and austerity (particularly at national and supranational governance levels).

Federalism and Interdependence

Resolving these tensions between top-down pressures for austerity, clarity, and control and bottom-up opportunities and demands for more participation and engagement requires a consideration of the workings of federalism, i.e., formalized jurisdictional boundaries separating levels of democratic authority (our primary focus in this book being countries such as Canada, the US, and Australia, though in keeping with above, it bears noting that the European Union is similarly a federalist variant of unique proportions extending across member countries). In a world of heightened complexity, traditional models of federalism premised upon separateness and jurisdictional clarity are under strain. While federalism remains a highly relevant and often desirable construct, its function and form must adapt to a more interdependent era (Langford and Roy 2008; Ubaldi and Roy 2010).

The argumentation of this book suggests that whereas national governments (and to a closely related degree, state and provincial governments built upon similar democratic structures) exhibit more hierarchical and top-down contours of decision-making, local governments are more varied in this regard, with greater degrees of freedom for participation experimentation of the sort more aligned with mobility and more open-source forms of democratic governance (to re-invoke the parlance of the previous chapter). A combination of demographic, economic, and technological agglomeration accompanying and closely intertwined with globalizing trends toward urbanization further reinforces the importance of local governments for cities (driving the sorts of experimentations examined in the previous chapter). Nevertheless, with respect to the federations most closely examined in this book—namely, Canada and the US (as well as Australia)—local governments are subordinate to higher-order levels without formalized constitutional recognition and the fiscal and operational autonomy that flows with it.

In short, nineteenth-century constitutions do not easily mesh with twenty-first-century realities. The costs from such a cleavage heighten considerably in virtual environments, much as they run counter to the very sorts of rhetorical promises routinely deployed by governments to become more adaptive and networked as policy complexity and administrative interdependence rise. Despite limited interest in service integration initiatives and better coordination across jurisdictions, for instance, there has been little equivalent debate in federalist countries such as the US and Canada as to whether a more fundamental redesign of federalist governance principles and arrangements is warranted (ibid.).

The centralizing tendencies of political leaders reflected (albeit to varying degrees given the structures shaping their relative power) in the Commander in Chief stature and evolving posture of President Obama and the omnibus budget bills of Prime Minister Harper are indicative in this regard (arguably more perverse and acute in the Canadian Parliamentary context given the largely unfettered legislative authority of a majority government). Such a characterization applies both within their national governing systems and across levels of government, despite both men having exhibited decentralist traits prior to taking office (Harper a longtime activist for Provincial rights and Obama a community organizer and subsequently a State legislator). Their national stature coupled with the fiscal and wider governance pressures for concentrated authority as leaders of countries is obviously a potential source of friction with the bottom-up flavor of online democratic experimentation in the preceding chapter.

Inspired by like-minded European challenges, Osimo articulates the need for more devolved forms of experimentation and adaptation, facilitated by a philosophy of "horizontal subsidiarity" (Osimo 2008). According to the author, moving in such a direction becomes increasingly feasible in a contemporary setting since: "One of the great advantages of Web 2.0 is that it lowers the cost of errors, as very little investment is needed to launch a collaboration..." (p. 47, ibid.). Paquet largely concurs with such a viewpoint, lamenting from the Canadian perspective the absence of a willingness to move in novel directions due to the engrained notions of traditionalism emphasizing competitiveness, separateness, and a close guarding of autonomy:

> Canada's brand of competitive formal federalism has proved capable of generating confusion, overlap, and counterproductive adversarialism. At the same time, the collaboration and partnering that are needed entail power sharing, and are often regarded as "unacceptable in principle" by the very organizations claiming to want to partner (Paquet 2001). So at a time when the amount and kind of collaboration required are deeper and richer than before, and there is a need for a greater variety of forums, reporting standards, and collaborative structures of a more permanent sort, these essential elements are often simply not there. (p. 13, Paquet 2004)

In keeping with Osimo's world view, Paquet thus calls for a new language and a new set of discursive mechanisms in order to explore the basis for collaboration and interdependence that must come to underwrite social learning and adaptive governance solutions less steeped in traditional boundaries than in experimental and flexible capacities (ibid., Dutil et al. 2010; Hubbard et al. 2012). Such directions are thus clearly more aligned with a mobility-laden environment than traditional federalist structures that view collaboration as the exception to the more pervasive norms of separation and jurisdictional control.

There is some evidence that such thinking has begun to pervade Australian governance modalities with respect to interactions across government levels. Firstly, collaborative and cross-jurisdictional governance arrangements have received considerable attention by both government leaders and academics relative to the aforementioned North American examples (Wanna and O'Flynn 2008). Secondly, a formal mechanism institutionalizing integrative and collaborative action across federal and state levels is in place: the Australian Council of Governments (this Council's focus on health care, for example, has yielded an integrative e-health scheme with notably more interdependence than Canadian and American likeminded initiatives thus far[5]). Thirdly, the creation of a national public body to foster the availability of high-speed, broadband infrastructure for communities of all sizes is a notable departure from the market-centric and more fragmented approaches of Canada and the US. Finally and closest to the focus of this book,

---

[5] See, for example, the National E-Health Transition Authority: http://www.nehta.gov.au/

the Australian federal government has formerly committed to stronger intergovernmental coordination in response to the recommendations of the Web 2.0 task force.[6] Indeed, more widely former Australian Prime Minister Kevin Rudd envisioned an era of more collaborative federalism where the Council of Australian Governments (comprising federal and state leaders) would serve as the engine of reform (Salusinszky 2012).

Yet traditionalism also pervades Australian efforts. The federal commitment to stronger e-government coordination across jurisdictions is general and without specifics, while a leading subnational example of a "Government 2.0 action plan" offered by the State of Victoria is notably devoid of new governance architectures enjoining these two government levels.[7] Accordingly, early efforts to devise plans and strategies for the pursuit of cloud computing solutions by governmental authorities in Australia have featured mainly separate exploration of such initiatives underway at each government level (even as the shared forums and dialogues sketched out above provide a basis for collaboration action).

Such tensions between traditional separateness and synergistic opportunities (and in some cases necessity) can only intensify. The advent of mobility demands more holistic and collaborative governance arrangements (akin to the networked principles and conduct of public value management) that encompass the public sector as a whole—both administratively and democratically. National governments in both federalist and non-federalist jurisdictions alike should view devolved experimentation as both an opportunity and necessity in terms of strengthening and innovating democratic governance models. The conundrum at present in many countries lies in how to foster a willingness to do so that does not threaten to diminish the perceived authority and control of those in office nationally. It is for this reason that any formalized process for democratic reform necessitates the combined impetus and support of all government levels in forging a neutral and independent mechanism to reexamine democratic structures holistically.

While recognizing the historically nurtured wisdom and stability of founding constitutional arrangements, it should not be a given that present federalist arrangements—stemming from an era of limited transportation infrastructure to say nothing of an absence of modern telecommunications and poorly educated and often disenfranchised citizenries—are best suited to an era of virtualization and mobility. As Fenna notes with respect to Australia but in a manner with relevance to most all federations today, it is already the case that the present degrees of policy complexity and overlapping issues and responsibilities vastly surpass what could have been initially foreseen when federalist structures were first devised (Fenna 2012).

---

[6]The formal government response was published on May 3, 2010: http://www.finance.gov.au/publications/govresponse20report/

[7]This strategy, however, denotes one of the richest examples of a digital and participatory governance strategy encompassing many central elements discussed through this book. Four guiding principles include leadership, participation, transparency, and performance. Source: http://www.egov.vic.gov.au/victorian-government-resources/government-2-0-action-plan/government-2-0-action-plan-victoria.html

Consequently, politicians and citizens alike must become much more knowledgeable and involved in technological design processes, especially in considering how best to invest in and maintain national digital infrastructures that enable rather than crowd out local experimentation. The aforementioned examples from Australia, for instance, along with the related formation of a 2009 Gov 2.0 Taskforce, have led to important political oxygen for such debates among not only the public and experts but elected officials themselves. One Australian Senator and Minister (Kate Lundy) thus can offer a well-informed commentary on many central themes and challenges pertaining to government's digital and participative adaptation and for cultivating the "foundations for open democracy" (Lundy 2010). While such pronouncements have yet to yield concrete reforms institutionally, they are nonetheless reflective of a more fertile environment for innovation and experimentation underpinned by likeminded, aforementioned initiatives such as the federal Gov 2.0 Taskforce and the State of Victoria's Gov 2.0 Action Plan that encompasses many key elements of openness discussed in preceding chapters.

As citizenries and political debates gravitate online—and as technological mobility facilitates an expansion of tools and processes for virtual interactions—the central and a yet unmet challenge for democracy lies in rebalancing representational mechanisms and more direct roles for public engagement on the one hand and in devising an alignment between in-person physicality and virtual spaces on the other. Once again drawing from the Australian context, participatory examples embedded within and led by civil society such as the 2020 Summit and the Citizen's Parliament are the sorts of initiatives meriting greater attention and resources—mixing grassroots involvement and formal expertise in ways decoupled from existing political institutions but with a mandate to improve them (Carson et al. 2011). Similarly, a global movement of localized initiatives for spurring open data and creating likeminded innovations in developing apps to make use of such openness reflects societal mobilization and the importance of local government: both are central to integrating and aligning virtualization with geographically based communities bound by spatial proximity.[8]

The implications of such movements for Australian federalism are mixed and intertwined with a political environment that remains largely traditional in terms of adversarial partisanship, particularly at the federal level where much like the Canadian and American contexts of late, there is growing cynicism and distrust of federal and state governments and their political leaders (Salusinszky 2012). Consistent with the argumentation of this chapter as well as its predecessor, however, there is some evidence to suggest that Australians are for the first time placing greater faith locally, viewed as the most effective level of government according to national surveys undertaken for a prominent academic study of federalism (ibid.).

In short, more than seeking to ordain and standardize change, national conversations must facilitate and nurture more localized initiatives, fostered partly online through virtual governance as well as more traditional community formations and venues.

---

[8] For more details of such initiatives, please see http://www.opendataday.org

Federalism cannot be neutral in this regard: it can either accentuate separateness and divisions or create conditions for innovative and collaborative renewal. Meaningful public engagement via more mobile democracy and public sector governance necessitates the latter.

The Government of Canada's Cloudy Expectations

An overriding theme of this book pertaining to Canada in one of laggardness in a manner that stands in stark contrast to the late 1990s, for example, when initial efforts to forge online government garnered recognition and praise from many domestic and international observers. In 2012, for example, Canada for the first time fell from the ten most highly rated nations in the UN Global E-Government Survey. When coupled with the many engrained degrees of administrative and political traditionalism associated with the traditional Westminster paradigm denoted as a machinery prism of governance, the resulting prospects for effectively embracing a mobility mindset become decidedly tempered. What explains this digital laggardness of recent years under Prime Minister Harper? In summarizing a number of elements invoked above, three considerations stand out.

Firstly, there is the overriding prism of the centralizing authority of the Prime Minister's Office and closely aligned central agencies that has long characterized Parliamentary governance and particularly so within the Canadian context (Clark and Swain 2005; Aucoin et al. 2011; Hubbard et al. 2012). In a manner reflective of some elements of the Ontario Premier's evolution discussed earlier in this chapter, Prime Minister Harper has introduced new mechanisms of openness and transparency with respect to ethics and accountability (largely as a response to spending scandals of the previous Liberal regime): yet these reforms have little to do with IT, while they have also been accompanied by strong countervailing pressures stemming from concentrated, hierarchical, and secretive authority (ibid.). In addition and as explained above, global economic uncertainty and the precarious fiscal environments of the neighboring US as well as much of Europe have reinforced a political calculus of strong and decisive economic stewardship mattering much more than democratic innovation and wider public engagement.

Secondly and further in keeping with one of the main themes of this chapter, namely, austerity, pressures to limit spending have translated into pressures to diminish the size of the federal public service mainly via program and workforce reductions (further accentuating secretive and centralizing tendencies in orchestrating a government-wide review to instigate such reductions). Within such a context, IT investments are largely framed as drivers of efficiency—more rooted within a mindset of consolidation and control rather than enablers of systemic reforms of the sorts likely to be more empowering and collaborative (a critical theme driving the evolution of present reforms to the federal government's IT architecture, a point returned to below).

Thirdly and once again in keeping with the other major theme of this chapter—namely, federalism—the Harper Government's conservative-leaning philosophy has led to a political and operational stance to be more overtly mindful of constitutional roles and boundaries between federal and provincial governments (municipalities falling under the domain of the latter group) and to thus limit the formalization of shared governance arrangements as much as practically possible.[9] This point, then, notably distinguishes Canadian federalism in recent years from the Australian variant which, by contrast, has featured a stronger dose of political collaboration across federal and state governments.

With respect to the evolution of digital infrastructure—and the consequences for the Canadian federal government, the overarching impact of these three directions has been to greatly limit the emergence of a web 2.0 and mobility laden mindset while instead reinforcing a more traditional cautious and control-minded stance toward IT investments and reform.

This point is evident symbolically with respect to the absence of a Cabinet-level champion of outward and participative-minded digital reform (of the sort personified by the Mayor of Calgary, for instance, or the aforementioned Senator Lundy of Australia). Tellingly, Tony Clement, a leading Conservative Minister in terms of social media usage and visibility in recent years while serving as Minister of Industry (which initially housed many early elements of the federal e-government architecture during the late 1990s and early 2000s) has since become President of the Treasury Board, resulting in a more inward, control-minded focus on the imposition of workforce and spending reductions. As noted in this book's introduction, by contrast, the social media presence of the federal government has instead come to be predominantly shaped by a Prime Ministerial apparatus focused on leveraging such new media channels within a linear and traditionally minded communications mindset emphasizing messaging (very much reflective of a traditional machinery-laden approach to partisan and information control).

The evolution of the Government of Canada's main service interface—Service Canada—is a further evidence of such inward and traditionalist-minded characterizations. Despite its online visibility as an information gateway to a variety of programs and services delivered by various federal departments and agencies, it has largely become administratively subsumed within its home department, Human Resource and Skills Development Canada (Roy 2012b). Not surprisingly, then, the federal government's inaugural pilot with respect to open data is administratively separate from Service Canada—despite the outwardly enabling purpose of this initiative spurring innovative usage of government information resources in ways that could presumably improve service processes (a key plan of open data initiatives in many jurisdictions). The housing of open data within the Treasury Board (the central agency responsible for operational and financial oversight—and the lead authority in overseeing expenditure and workforce reductions) instead suggests misalignment and a very limited appetite for participative engagement and experimentation.

---

[9] Prime Minister Harper has thus largely refused to attend First Minister's meetings, for example, comprising Provincial Premiers and Territorial leaders.

Consequently and in contrast to the rhetoric of many observers both inside and outside of government calling for an exploration of a Service 2.0 mindset—featuring greater public involvement in both evaluating and designing service offerings[10] (and thus emblematic of open data)—there is little evidence of any meaningful governance capacity to pursue such collaborative and participative aims (ibid.). This characterization holds true externally with respect to new forms of public engagement, much as it also applies to internal public sector reforms engineered in a tightly orchestrated and efficiency-driven manner.[11]

Within this incrementally minded context of efficiency and control, the most significant and like-minded digital initiative of recent years, taking shape in 2012, is the formation of Shared Services Canada (SSC), as distinct from the aforementioned, Service Canada. Unlike Service Canada, SSC would receive new legislative underpinnings in 2012 giving this new agency autonomy and formal authority to undertake government-wide initiatives in terms of refurbishments to the digital infrastructure at the federal level. Central to this refurbishment are the interrelated variables of consolidation and cloud computing: the former viewed as an efficiency source in moving to more integrated, shared electronic platforms and the latter a presumably strategic option reflecting the evolution of digital governance systems the world over.

With respect to this latter point, the opportunities and complexities and risks of cloud computing were examined in Chap. 4, drawing upon a number of public sector initiatives undertaken to explore them. Prominent among such initiatives are the Government of Australia's cloud computing framework and that of Singapore to name but two: the US federal government's latest strategy for digital and mobile government (examined in Chap. 5) similarly based upon a high degree of organizational investment into cloud computing options during the first Obama mandate, yielding a number of specific initiatives. All of themes initiative have in common a public commitment to the exploration of cloud-based systems, including recognition of the risks (and potential opportunities) surrounding privacy and security that accompany them.

SSC, by contrast, is framed primarily as an initiative premised upon consolidation as its main objective. The Minister responsible for SSC has publicly lauded the initiative as groundbreaking in this regard, pointing to the consolidation and integration of email systems and data centers as key initiatives. Yet despite widespread recognition by both government and industry managers involved in moving such initiatives forward that the options ahead invariably involve at least an exploration of cloud computing as an option, this term is nowhere to be found on the website of SCC (as of the end of 2012).[12]

---

[10] See, for example, Flumian's quote reservice codesign and prosumers in Chap. 2.

[11] In accordance with this characterization, the federal open data effort is housed within the confines of Treasury Board, the central agency responsible for financial and managerial oversight of the Government of Canada including government-wide expenditure reviews (also housing, albeit awkwardly in this regard, the government-wide CIO Office).

[12] This observation includes the publicly available Integrated Business Plan for 2012–2013 as well as entering the term "cloud" in the search function of the SSC home page.

The main lesson here is not to prejudge the degree to which cloud computing should be deployed going forward, but rather to underscore that its absence from the public discourse surrounding digital infrastructure adaptation going forward is striking. Not surprisingly, then, such an absence is increasingly noticed as highlighted by an online article published by Forbes in November 2012 entitled "The Sorry State of Cloud Computing in Canada" (Cohen 2012). Perhaps in response to such widening critiques, SSC did announce in late 2012 the formation of a new round table with industry stakeholders that can unavoidably be expected to result in the tabling of cloud computing as one issue under its domain moving ahead.

Such trepidation on the part of the federal government (reinforced by escalating cybersecurity and data-breach concerns that, paradoxically, increase the value and importance of a strategic and political dialogue on cloud computing) should not entirely mask the significant municipal and provincial experimentation building across the country and the potential for bottom-up renewal of the sort characterizing experimentation with engagement (as discussed in the previous chapter). It does, however, expose a significant cleavage between the potential to explore federated architectures for the public sector as a whole (since the very nature of cloud computing is conducive to such shared virtualization) and the current top-down orientation of political federalism and the apparent inability and unwillingness of the federal (i.e., central) government to orchestrate collective action in this regard.

As discussed in the preceding section, while decentralized and localized innovation can be an important basis for eventually renewing federal government priorities and initiatives, the significant scope of federal IT spending and the media and public visibility of federal initiatives are an equally important variable in shaping the public sector's holistic evolution in terms of both back-end infrastructure and frontline performance. Moreover, the overriding inward and cautionary tendencies of the federal government in terms of IT architectures and governance clearly reinforce a machinery-laden mindset of government as opposed to more mobility-oriented visions and governance reforms that more readily associate concepts such as cloud computing and social media with an alternative and more open and participative mindset.

The cultural and structural cleavage between machinery and mobility is thus widened rather than narrowed, a point underscored not only by the actions and priorities of Ministers and entities such as the federal agency, SSC, but also by the absence of political and public dialogues on such matters more generally. In contrast, for example, to UK Parliamentary Committees that routinely scrutinize governmental actions in this regard—conducting hearings and reporting to the citizenry and stakeholders accordingly—the legislative branch of the federal Parliament of Canada has been stunningly absent on such matters specifically in terms of government initiatives as well as public engagement more widely with respect to the longer-term evolution of democracy and public management (a key point also invoked in terms of privacy and citizenship matters discussed in Chap. 6).

In sum, at present the Government of Canada would seem to be exhibiting many of the tendencies of a machinery-laden bureaucracy, highly cautious toward mobility, and like-minded governance innovation predicated on more openness and wider engagement. As with the Ontario example, many provinces, sharing common Westminster foundations, have found transiting away from tradition to be a similarly stunted and cautionary path (although certainly there is a widening provincial experimentation in many aspects of governance reform discussed through this book: initiatives toward openness and engagement undertaken by the Province of British Columbia, for example, are less developed though akin in some respects to the State of Victoria's efforts in Australia[13]).

Such traditionalism greatly constrains the localism of community and municipal endeavors and suggests that Canada as a country risks lagging further behind in many aspects of digital governance and political innovation relative to a growing number of its counterparts internationally. Stepping back from Canadian specifics but certainly relevant to the plight of this country in this regard, the book's conclusion seeks both a summation of the main challenges and points of tension confronting the public sector in a participative age and a presentation of the major contours of reform that must be pursued looking ahead.

---

[13] BC is the first Canadian Province to publish its own "Gov 2.0" strategy, available here: http://www.gov.bc.ca/citz/citizens_engagement/gov20.pdf

Conclusion

Mobility and V.O.I.C.E

The many issues and challenges examined through the preceding chapters are enjoined by a fundamental mobility imperative that cannot be ignored: the set of choices being not whether to adapt but rather in terms of the pace and specifics of doing so. For the time being, there is something of a core-peripheral dichotomy to such change and adaptation at present: many jurisdictions feature a widening array of peripheral, grassroots, often-localized, and incremental innovations, whereas many of the core structures and cultural principles of democratic power and conduct remain largely unaltered (and in some cases reinforced, particularly from a national vantage point).

The reality is that the gravitational inertia of traditional government machinery remains strong, increasingly challenged, and under strain but also reinforced by historical custom on the one hand and an interrelated set of technological and political forces seeking greater clarity and control in an uncertain (and for some unsettling) environment. More so than in the marketplace (where creative destructionism is often celebrated), the stability premium of the state can, at times, reflect a wider consideration of viewpoints and perspectives in an institutional setting meant to be inclusive in execution and legitimate in perception. Accordingly, public office holders regularly laud and pledge allegiance to constitutions and symbols and institutional structures created centuries ago, and indeed this unifying logic of state power and identity is an important distinguishing feature between stable democracies (where in most cases at least, parties and political leaders come and go) and aspiring ones where democratic power is contested in more volatile and even violent ways (as stability is obviously of central and defining importance in nondemocratic systems as well).

Notwithstanding important variants between Parliamentary and Presidential regimes, this penchant for stability has infused public administration with long-standing hierarchical-laden values of deference to elected authority—underpinned by stable employment tenures to offset electorally driven turnover which, it bears

J. Roy, *From Machinery to Mobility: Government and Democracy in a Participative Age*, 111
Public Administration and Information Technology 2, DOI 10.1007/978-1-4614-7221-6,
© Springer Science+Business Media New York 2013

noting, has no obvious comparator in the private sector. In addition, public servants have traditionally been shielded from visibility and direct responsibility, with politicians said to be solely assuming of such duties (particularly in the Westminster Parliamentary model). While justifiable within a strictly traditional reading of the machinery of government and its cornerstone principle of Ministerial accountability, there is already an important convergence between mobility-inspired models of more open and participatory governance and the more complex functioning and organization of contemporary public sector governance systems featuring an array of corporate governance mechanisms, independent offices, and collaborative arrangements.

Accordingly, public value management and like-minded networked and participatory-driven schools of thought are more welcoming of what are already undeniable characteristics of a new governance order: "openness, participation, and collaboration" to borrow the three pillars of the 2009 Obama Openness Directive or the four pillars of the comprehensive "Gov 2.0 Action Plan" of the Australian State of Victoria (leadership, participation, transparency, performance) noted in the previous chapter. More than the early days of e-government that often preserved many core elements of traditional government (and added elements of new public management), the mobility era more firmly entrenches the need for public value management and like-minded perspectives as a basis for a set of governance principles embracing open collaboration and complexity and infused with participative learning and constant adaptation (Dutil et al. 2010; Maier-Rabler and Huber 2011; Reddick and Aikins 2012; Hubbard et al. 2012; Lips 2012).

Within a set of parameters that remain contested and fluid but at the very least are identifiable as a basis for constructive deliberation and reform, any effective design (or redesigning) of public sector governance requires a solid understanding of the main sources of tension not only administratively and politically but also socially and technologically.

In my estimation, then, the distinguishing feature of democratic and public sector governance in the mobile age is the need *to give voice* to a wider array of citizens and stakeholders both within and outside of government in ways that infuse both political and administrative processes with more active and ongoing participative elements. These participative elements are the basis of upfront innovation, informed and collaborative judgments about results and outcomes, and the centrally important aspects of learning and adaptive accountability in between.

By way of summation with respect to the critical themes of this book, V.O.I.C.E also constitutes a useful acronym for presenting the set of design tensions that must be both recognized and reconciled in going forward:

- *Virtual:* the widening implantation of a Web 2.0 ethos of active participation driven by online activity generally, social media specifically, as well as a proliferation of mobile devices and wireless connectivity that greatly expands opportunities for virtualization both within the workplace and across society more widely

  - Nonetheless, the bureaucratic foundations of the public sector that emphasize process and control reinforce proximate spatial patterns in structuring organizations and a persistent reliance on paper-based processing.

- *Open*: the rise of open-source software and cloud infrastructure models, heightened demands for both proactive and reactive forms of transparency, and a widening ethos of collaborative openness as the basis of shared innovation and value creation in an increasingly networked environment

  - Nonetheless, governments (and significant segments of industry) remain strongly attached to viewing information and knowledge holdings as proprietary concepts, and secrecy remains at the core of most representational democratic regimes.

- *Intermediation*: traditional forms of corporate and professionalized media intermediation are increasingly rivalled by new forms of social media creating opportunities for more directly informing and involving the public in democratic governance

  - Nonetheless, new filters and mechanisms must be forged both institutionally and technologically in order to preserve and renew the discursive dimension to democratic discourse and conduct that otherwise risks becoming more fragmented and adversarial.

- *Collaboration*: widespread collaboration at the heart of Web 2.0 and Gov 2.0 driving the logic of participative value creation and the pursuit and usage of collective intelligence

  - Nonetheless, democratic architectures and traditional public administration remain predicated on hierarchical and informational control.

- *Engagement*: citizens increasingly informed, educated, and technologically enabled to partake in democratic discourse and more participative governance models seeking to mobilize and leverage new sources and forms of collective intelligence

  - Nonetheless, the overarching customer logic emphasizes choice and self-interest at the expense of responsibility and collective action, intensifying the commercialization and individualization of political culture within formal democratic institutions.

Some readers may enjoin the beginning and ending of this acronym (i.e., virtual and engaged) with a sharper emphasis on digital divide matters than has afforded by this book (e.g., notwithstanding its centrality to Chap. 6). If this important issue has been somewhat downplayed, it is due mainly to the premise that technologically, mobility is at the very least a potential enabler of greater inclusiveness: less costly and increasingly powerful mobile devices on the one hand and a widening range of new innovations on the other hand to lessen physical and cognitive handicaps underpin the potential for digital societies to become more inclusive ones. Albeit unevenly (due to widely varying conditions across different parts of the world), such potential consistently emerges from the UN's own Global E-Government Surveys, for example. Yet it must also be acknowledged that this global cataloguing and accompanying analysis also demonstrates the manner by which technology alone cannot suffice in surmounting existing divides that encompass a complex set of socioeconomic variables.

In the developed world, by contrast (and the focus of this book), countries ranging from Scandinavian nations to Singapore and South Korea (and to some degree Australia with its national broadband initiative) have sought to create the conditions for widespread if not ubiquitous coverage of online infrastructure. The most pertinent questions that persist within such nations, and much of the OECD world, pertain to the willingness of citizens to engage, the opportunities and obligations for doing so, and the ability of the public sector to orchestrate participation toward discursive and collective outcomes. Previous chapters have sought to provide some guidance as to how this orchestration can ideally be pursued—first and foremost as a localized project—while acknowledging the overriding importance and impacts of national systems and the need for holistic redress across an evermore enjoined set of multilayered governance arrangements both administratively and politically.

The key challenge, then, for national governments is to find ways to become an enabler of mobile adaptation rather than a barrier standing in such a path, both in terms of its own functioning as a set of organizational and institutional arrangements and as a model for a more networked governance order for the jurisdiction as a whole. In accordance with the V.O.I.C.E doctrine presented above, prescriptive solutions for change and renewal—to carry legitimacy and meaningful impact—must themselves be open sourced and collaborative in formation.

Change from Within

To be more open to changes taking place outside, governments must do more to foster innovation from within. An important starting point, therefore, in seeking genuine public engagement is to meaningfully empower and engage employees internally—in manners favoring agility and innovation over anonymity and risk aversion. Building on the considerable experimentation that already exists—much of it already engineered by public servants—a central tenant in transiting to a new governance order, in shifting from machinery to mobility, is to foster a more participatory ethos channeling collaborative and shared action into performance-minded governance mechanisms considerably less constrained by process and control.

This fundamental shift includes managerial, technological, organizational, and political dimensions.

Managerially, the fundamental challenge is breaking free from the mindset of both clarity and physicality that define the traditional office environment and shape work processes and practices in accordance with bureaucratic foundations. There is no greater vice on the inability of the public sector to enable empowerment and to focus on results—and the era of mainframe systems and desktop computers largely reinforced such control-laden tendencies. More disconcerting still, in the absence of an alternative managerial mindset, layering mobile devices and online platforms upon hierarchical structures merely accentuates information overload and heightens the stress and frustration stemming from the cleavage between recognizing the potential for doing things differently and the constraints of existing and engrained approaches (a cleavage closely interrelated with demographics and evolving government capacities for recruitment and retention as first discussed in Chap. 2).

Technologically, such an alternative, mobility-inspired mindset means that what matters more than the creation of a Chief Mobility Officer or like-minded czar to ordain such changes are mechanisms to enjoin the multitude of grassroots initiatives underway across the public sector. BYOD (bring your own device) is indicative of such flexibility, though truly mobile organizations would not require the "bringing" of a device to a virtual workplace inclusive of the home, remote locations, and common office spaces. As discussed in Chap. 3, effectively migrating to such mobility platforms and tools demands flexibility and empowerment in order to facilitate creativity and productivity improvement—rather than extending the shackles of bureaucratic control from a nine-to-five workspace to the one always on, twenty-four seven. In an increasingly cloud-enabled and participative environment, governments will be challenged to abandon traditional procurement models emphasizing secrecy and proprietary protection in favor of a suite of standards and options appropriately tailored to the mission of scope of individual units. A culture of mobility requires constant dialogue across government not to ordain decisions and choices across the public sector but rather to facilitate more informed decision-making, greater sensitivity to risks surrounding privacy and security, and above all else heightened degrees of freedom to deploy new technologies toward innovative and collaborative objectives.

Organizationally, a more participative and mobile mindset necessitates the creation of organizational structures more networked and adaptable than rigidly hierarchical. Such agility is particularly important in orchestrating collaborative action in light of unanticipated crises and increasingly complex policy and service demands (Lips 2012). Yet digital government has instead often stymied such innovation due to the re-assertive nature of the traditional public administration mindset of bureaucratic centralizing that has sought deeper planning and resources on a government-wide scale. Mobility necessitates a delicate balancing of coordinating mechanisms and empowering capacities, the latter aligned with a participative performance-minded culture. It is both unavoidable and beneficial that senior public servants be on the frontlines of devising such a balance, visible and accountable and increasingly well versed in virtual realities.

Politically, such managerial, technological, and organizational experimentation—all more open, collaborative, and participative—can only succeed if the workings and interactions of elected officials are amendable and appropriately aligned. A culture of internal and external engagement can only take hold if elected officials behave in similar manners, meaning new forms of collaborative power-sharing and openness in stark contrast to the traditions of secrecy and information control. This is, without question, a tall order given the fact that those occupying elected offices today succeeded in doing so by mastering the rules of existing institutional architectures rather than envisioning new ones. Elements of a more participatory and less partisan political culture are nevertheless emerging—particularly across localities, as we have seen, but also within even the most polarized and adversarial political theaters of late, Washington, DC.[1]

Yet deeper structural and stylistic reforms are also required. Although their exploration can and must be supported by those in government, renewed democratic legitimacy must itself be an open, collective, and participatory endeavor. In accordance and in concert with a more informed and participative society—and thus citizenry—new and more independent public mechanisms are required in order to facilitate the transition to a new democratic order less rooted in a machinery-laden representational model and more open and participatory.

From Commissions to Crowd-Sourcing

This sort of mechanism may be thought of in a manner akin to Royal and Presidential Commissions of the past—within their top-heavy reliance on respected public figures and outsourced expertise (often with a limited consultative element alongside). By contrast, democracies today require a bold crowd-sourcing of democratic renewal by aligning widespread participation and ownership on the one hand and discursive processes on the other hand. Such a shift from open data toward open democracy may be presented to the public as a rare and unique opportunity to overcome cynicism and narrow self-interests and chart a new course for politics and government. While the main contours of debate surrounding this new course are sketched out above, it must again be underscored that in order for such an inherently open-sourced process to succeed, its parameters and ultimate findings cannot be preordained in any specific manner: it instead must be the product of novel ways to leverage collective intelligence.

Appropriately situated at the center of the V.O.I.C.E. acronym, literally and figuratively, the notion of "open" is without question central to both the transformation that lies ahead as well as the continuing and embedded resistance of many actors both inside and outside of government. This is so due to the secretive ethos at the heart of representational democracy and its resulting pressures for partisan and hierarchical control. Akin to tensions between open source and proprietary protection in the marketplace, struggles surrounding the ownership of both information and ideas are central to the tension between machinery and mobility even as the argumentation of this book suggests an irreversible—albeit contested—course toward the spreading of openness as a deepening governance principle.

---

[1] In January 2013 former Republican Senator Jon Huntsman and current Democratic Senator Joe Manchin announced the formation of a new entity entitled No Labels (http://www.nolabels.org) meant to spur bipartisan and less partisan policy dialogues both within Congress and across the citizenry: the launching of this new movement features a rich array of online resources including social media channels in order to instigate change from both within existing institutions and in grassroots manners. While the ramifications of one such initiative may well prove limited, a key lesson of Chap. 7 worthy of reiteration here is that a more deliberative and participative polity requires less partisanship and more political innovation of this sort.

Debates and choices concerning privacy are illustrative. Shaped by the commercialization logic of the marketplace, government managers and politicians often speak of trade-offs between convenience and privacy—whereas the more crucial set of trade-offs for democracy and public administration arguably lie within the inter-relationship between citizenship and privacy, in line with Young's call for a culture of "data activism" discussed in Chap. 6. Importantly, younger people embrace openness in ways that are both encouraging and distressing: the former in keeping with the basis of shared and participative governance systems that are predicated upon more systemic openness and the latter in what can often be an excessive disregard for legitimate forms of proprietary protection and like-minded privacy matters with respect to their own personal information and identity. Resolving such tensions in a deliberative manner represents a central societal project just beginning to take shape—with critical ramifications for the organization and conduct of democratic governance.

In short, shifting from machinery to mobility is both a digital and demographic imperative that must be built upon a new narrative forged in large measure by today's youth (i.e., tomorrow's generations of managers, elected officials, entrepreneurs, and activists). The challenge for current political leaders is not to ordain such a narrative—but rather to inject within and alongside present institutions the conditions and oxygen for such a dialogue to strengthen and ultimately deliver a collective blueprint for the genuine renewal of democratic governance.

Bibliography

Accenture. (2009). *Web 2.0 and the next generation of public service: Driving high performance through cloud.* Accenture.

Allegretti, G. (2011). From scepticism to mutual support: Towards a structural change in the relations between participatory budgeting and the information and communications technologies?. In P. Mindus, A. Greppi, M. Cuono (Eds.), *Legitimacy 2.0: E-democracy and public opinion in the digital age.* Selected papers from the IVR World Congress Special Workshop, Frankfurt. http://www.academiia.edu

Alzner, B. (2012). *Newfoundland passes Bill 29 to amend access to Information legislation.* The Canadian Journalism Project. Retrieved from: http://j-source.ca/article/newfoundland-passes-bill-29-amend-access-information-legislation

Andoh-Baidoo, F. K., Amoako-Gyampah, K., & Osei-Bryson, K.-M. (2010). How internet security breaches harm market value. *IEEE Security & Privacy, 8*(1), 36–42.

Ashlie, T. (2011). So how will I pay my housekeeper? Cheque elimination—The top 10 issues. *Forum, Canadian Payments Association, 27*(4), 12–13.

Aucoin, P., Jarvis, M., & Turnbull, L. (2011). *Democratizing the constitution: Reforming responsible government.* Toronto, ON: Emond Montgomery Publications.

Bamford, J. (2012). *The NSA is building the country's biggest spy center (Watch What You Say).* Retrieved from Wired: http://www.wired.com/threatlevel/2012/03/ff_nsadatacenter/all/

Batorski, M., & Hadden, D. (2010) Embracing Government 2.0. Virginia: Grant Thorton. Retrieved from: http://www.grantthornton.com/staticfiles/GTCom/Public sector/Gov20Jan2010.pdf

Belanger, D., Coe, A., & Roy, J. (2007). *Why business models matter. CIO Government Review* (July), IT World Canada.

Bermonte, A. (2011). Senior leaders' use of web 2.0 and social media in the Ontario Public Service (2011). *Theses and dissertations.* Paper 680, Ryerson University, Toronto. http://digitalcommons.ryerson.ca/dissertations/680

Bertot, J. C., Jaeger, P., & Grimes, J. (2010a). Using ICTs to create a culture of transparency: E-government and social media as openness and anti-corruption tools for societies. *Government Information Quarterly, 27,* 264–271.

Bertot, J. C., Jaeger, P., Munson, S., & Glaisyer, T. (2010b). Social media technology and government transparency. *IEEE Computer Society, 43,* 53–59.

Birch, J. (2008). Nanaimo's GOOGLE experience. *Municipal World, 118*(6), 5–9.

Blakemore, M., & Lloyd, P. (2007). *Think Paper 10. Trust and transparency: Pre-requisites for effective eGovernment.* cc:eGov Organisational Change for Citizen-centric eGovernment.

Borins, S., Kernaghan, K., Brown, D., Bontis, N., 6, P., & Thompson, F. (2007). *Digital State at the Leading Edge.* Toronto: University of Toronto Press. http://www.amazon.ca/Digital-State-at-Leading-Edge/dp/0802094902#reader_0802094902

Buckler, G., & Majer, A. (2008). *Mobile government: Governance and government in the age of mobility.* Toronto, ON: New Paradigm (now nGenera Corporation Canada).

Cain, S. (2012). *Quiet: The power of introverts in a world that can't stop talking.* New York: Crown.

Canadian Bankers Association. (2012, November 9). *How Canadians bank.* Retrieved from Canadian Bankers Association:http://www.cba.ca/en/media-room/50-backgrounders-on-banking-issues/125-technology-and-banking

Carmody, T. (2012, February 24). Apple gives shareholders more input: Will Facebook get the message? *WIRED Magazine.*

Carr, N. (2008). *Is Google Making Us Stupid?* Retrieved from The Atlantic: http://www.theatlantic.com/magazine/archive/2008/07/is-google-making-us-stupid/306868/

Carr, N. G. (2010). *The shallows: What the internet is doing to our brains.* New York: W. W. Norton.

Carr-West, J. (2009). From e-democracy to 'here comes everybody' a short history of government and the internet. In A. Sawford (Ed.), *Local government 3.0: How councils can respond to the new web agenda* (pp. 4–9). London: Local Government Information Unit.

Carson, L., Gastil, J., Hartz-Karp, J., & Lubensky, R. (Eds.). (2011). *The Australian citizens' parliament and the future of deliberative democracy.* University Park, PA: Pennsylvania State University Press.

CBC News. (2012). *N.S. civil servants refuse to relocate.* Retrieved online: http://www.cbc.ca/news/canada/nova-scotia/story/2012/05/11/ns-relocation-refusal-jessome.html

Charalabidis, Y., Loukis, E., & Kleinfeld, R. (2012). Towards a rationalisation of social media exploitation in government policy-making processes. *European Journal of ePractice, 16,* 77–93.

Clark, I., & Swain, H. (2005). Distinguishing the real from the surreal in management reform: Suggestions for beleaguered administrators in the government of Canada. *Canadian Public Administration, 48*(4), 453–476.

Clemens, J., & Crowley, B. L. (2012). *Solutions to critical infrastructure problems: Essays on protecting Canada's infrastructure.* Ottawa, ON: The MacDonald—Laurier Institute.

Coe, A., Paquet, G., & Roy, J. (2001). E-governance and smart communities: A social learning challenge. *Social Science Computer Review, 19*(1), 80–93.

Cohen, R. (2012). *The sorry state of cloud computing in Canada.* Retrieved from Forbes: http://www.forbes.com/sites/reuvencohen/2012/10/24/the-sorry-state-of-cloud-computing-in-canada/

Collier, D. (2011). *Cloud computing 201: Guidelines for successful cloud investments.* Washington, DC: CAGW.

Conabree, D. (2011). Intellectual capital and e-collaboration: The hidden cost of the status quo. *Fmi Journal, 23*(1), 11–12.

Cornish, P. (2009). *Cyber security and politically, socially and religiously motivated cyber attacks.* Brussels: Directorate-General for External Policies of the Union Directorate Policy Department. European Parliament.

CSC. (2011). *Ahead in the cloud: The CSC cloud usage index.* CSC. Retrieved from: http://assets1.csc.com/newsroom/downloads/CSC_Cloud_Usage_Index.pdf

Dahlgren, P. (2005). The Internet, public spheres, and political communication: Dispersion and deliberation. *Political Communication, 22,* 147–162.

Danske Bank. (2011). *Press conference annual report 2010.* Danske bank. http://www.danske-bank.com

de Jong, A. (2011). *Benefits of cloud computing realized by increasing number of companies.* Retrieved from Cloud Times: http://cloudtimes.org/2011/08/27/benefits-of-cloud-computing-realized-by-increasing-number-of-companies/

Dean, D., & Webb, C. (2011). Recovering from information overload. *McKinsey Quarterly.*

Dunleavy, P., Margetts, H., Bastow, S., & Tinkler, J. (2006). New public management is dead—Long live digital-era governance. *Journal of Public Administration Research and Theory, 16*(3), 467–494.

Dutil, P., Howard, C., Langford, J., & Roy, J. (2010). *The service state—Rhetoric, reality, and promise* (Governance series). Ottawa, ON: University of Ottawa Press.

Dutton, W. H., & Peltu, M. (2007). *Reconfiguring government–public engagements: enhancing the communicative power of citizens* (Forum Discussion Paper No. 9). Oxford Internet Institute.

Duxbury, L., & Higgins, C. (2012). *Revisiting Work-Life Issues in Canada: The 2012 National Study on Balancing Work and Caregiving in Canada.* Ottawa, ON: Carleton University & The University of Western Ontario. Retrieved from: http://www.healthyworkplaces.info/wp-content/uploads/2012/11/2012-National-Work-Long-Summary.pdf

Eaves, D. (2009). *MuniForge: Creating municipalities that work like the web.* Retrieved online: http://eaves.ca/2009/12/08/muniforge-creating-municipalities-that-work-like-the-web/

Economist Intelligence Unit (2006) Foresight 2020 – Economic, industry and corporate trends (chapter two: public sector).

Eger, J. M. (2012). *The creative community: Meeting the challenges of the new economy.* San Diego, CA: CreateSpace Independent Publishing Platform.

Eggers, W. (2005). *Government 2.0: Using technology to improve education, cut red tape, reduce gridlock and enhance democracy.* New York: Rowman and Littlefield Publishers.

Fatland, E. (2007). *Democratic interfaces: Decision-making tools for online communities.* MA thesis, Media Lab University of Arts and Design, Helsinki.

Fenna, A. (2012). *Intergovernmental grants and accountability in Australian federalism.* COAG Reform Council. Retrieved from: http://www.coagreformcouncil.gov.au/excellence/docs/events/Think_piece_Fenna_2012.pdf

Florida, R. (2005). *The flight of the creative class: The new global competition for talent.* New York: Reed Business Information.

Flumian, M. (2009). *Citizens as prosumers: the next frontier of service innovation.* Ottawa, ON: nGenera Institute on Governance.

Flumian, M., Coe, A. A., & Kernaghan, K. (2007). Transforming service to Canadians: The service Canada model. *International Review of Adminstrative Sciences, 73*(4), 557–568.

Fountain, J. E. (2001). *Building the virtual state: Information technology and institutional change.* Washington, DC: Brookings Institution Press.

Friedman T. (2011, October 23) Info technology revolution is taking off big-time. Retrieved from The Daily Advance: http://www.dailyadvance.com/opinion/other-views/thomas-friedman-infotechnology-revolution-taking-big-time-734597

Fyfe, T., & Crookall, P. (2010). *Social media and public sector policy dilemma.* Toronto, ON: IPAC.

Giggey, R. (2011, May 7). The G4: Setting city data free. *Canadian Government Executive, 17*(8). Retrieved from: http://www.canadiangovernmentexecutive.ca/category/item/152.html

Gladwell, M. (2010, October 4). Small change—Why this revolution will not be tweeted. *The New Yorker*

Goldsmith, J., & Hathaway, M. (2010). The cyber security changes we need. *The Washington Post.*

Gooderham, M. (2012). *Digital wallet slow to gain acceptance.* Retrieved from The Globe and Mail: http://www.theglobeandmail.com/globe-investor/personal-finance/financial-road-map/digital-wallet-slow-to-gain-acceptance/article2414790/?from=sec501

Goodyear, M., Goerdel, H. T., Portillo, S., & Williams, L. (2010). *Cybersecurity management in the states: The emerging role of chief information security officers.* Washington, DC: IBM Center for The Business of Government.

Greenwood, G. (2012). *Probing Obama's secrecy games: Will high-level Obama officials who leak for political gain be punished on equal terms with actual whistleblowers?* Retrieved from Salon: http://www.salon.com/2012/06/07/probing_obamas_secrecy_games/

Gupta, U. (2010). *Wanted 10,000 New Cybersecurity Pros: US Cyber Challenge Kicks Off Nationwide Talent Search.* Bank Info Security. Retrieved from: http://www.bankinfosecurity.com/wanted-10000-new-cybersecurity-pros-a-2597

Habermas, J. (2011). *Europe's post-democratic era.* Retrieved from the guardian: http://www.guardian.co.uk/commentisfree/2011/nov/10/jurgen-habermas-europe-post-democratic

Hamel, G., & Breen, B. (2007). *The Future of Management.* Cambridge, MA: Harvard Business School Press.

Hardin, G. (1968). The tragedy of the commons. *Science, 162*(3859), 1243–1248.

Hardy, B., Graham, R., Stansall, P., White, A., Harrison, A., Bell, A., et al. (2008). *Working beyond walls: The government workplace as an agent of change*. London: DEGW/OGC.

HealthForceOntario (2011). *Social Media*. Toronto, ON: HealthForceOntario: Marketing and Recruitment Agency. Retrieved from: https://www.healthforceontario.ca/ru/pdfs/RU_SMEDIA.pdf

Helbig, N., Cresswell, A. M., Burke, G., & Luna-Reyes, L. (2012). *The Dynamics of Opening Government Data: A White Paper*. Center for Technology in Government: Albany http://www.ctg.albany.edu.

Hubbard, R., Paquet, G., & Wilson, C. (2012). *Stewardship: Collaborative metagovernance and inquiring systems*. Ottawa, ON: Invenire Books.

Hull, R. T. (1979). *The varieties of ethical theories*. Buffalo, NY: Buffalo Psychiatric Centre.

Indvik, L. (2011). *5 Big trends in mobile commerce*. Retrieved from Mashable: http://mashable.com/2011/06/21/mobile-commerce-trends/

INSA. (2009). *Addressing cyber security through public-private partnership: An analysis of existing models*. Washinton, DC: Intelligence and National Security Alliance (INSA).

Irvine, C. E., & Palmer, C. C. (2010). Call in the cyber national guard! *IEEE Security & Privacy, 8*(1), 56–59.

Kamarck, E. C. (2002). *Applying 21st century government to homeland security*. Arlington, VA: PricewaterhouseCoopers Endowment for the Business of Government.

Kernaghan, K. (2013). Helping yourself: Changing the channel on public sector services. *Canadian Government Executive, 18*(10). Retrieved from: http://www.canadiangovernmentexecutive.ca/category/item/1101-helping-yourself-changing-the-channel-on-public-sector-services.html

Kernaghan, K., & Langford, J. (1990). *The responsible public servant*. Toronto, ON: Institute for Public Administration of Canada.

Kettl, D. (2005). *The next government of the United States: Challenges for performance in the 21st century*. Washington, DC: IBM Center for the Business of Government.

Kingwell, M. (2010). *The shout doctrine. Walrus magazine*. Toronto, ON: Walrus Foundation.

Kiss, J. (2010). *G-cloud would help government save*. Retrieved from The Guardian: http://www.guardian.co.uk/cloud-computing/g-cloud-would-help-the-government-to-save

Knowles, M. S. (1990). *The adult learner*. Burlington, MA: Elsevier.

Kostakis, V. (2011). The advent of open source democracy and wikipolitics: Challenges, threats and opportunities for democratic discourse. *An Interdisciplinary Journal on Human in ICT Environment, 7*(1), 9–29.

Kotsiopoulos, I. (2009). *Bringing together and accelerating eGovernment research in the EU: eDemocracy report*. ICT for Government and Public Services Unit, European Commission.

Kovar, J. F. (2011). *Former U.S. CIO Kundra Outlines Behind-The-Curtain IT Reorganization*. Retrieved from CRN: http://www.crn.com/news/data-center/231900783/former-u-s-cio-kundra-outlines-behind-the-curtain-it-reorganization.htm;jsessionid=H6Tik+zFpPOmF+4i1kt zFw**.ecappj03

Kraemer, K. L., & King, J. L. (2005). Information technology and administrative reform: Will E-government be different? *International Journal of Electronic Government, 2*(1), 1–20.

Kwon, K. (2012). *South Korea's 'Best of the Best' tackle cyber crime*. Retrieved from CNN: http://edition.cnn.com/2013/01/14/world/asia/south-korea-hackers/index.html

Lacigova, O., Maizite, A., & Cave, B. (2012). eParticipation and Social Media: a Symbiotic Relationship? *European Journal of ePractice, 16*, 71–76.

Lake, A. (2011). *The SmartWorking Handbook: How to reduce costs and improve business performance through new ways of working—A practical guide*. London: fexibility.co.uk. Retrieved from: http://docs.media.bitpipe.com/io_10x/io_100895/item_431149/SmartWorking %20Handbook_final2.pdf

Lane, G., & Roy, J. (2011). Mobility and government: How to MEET the challenge. *Canadian Government Executive, 17*(8). Retrieved from: http://www.canadiangovernmentexecutive.ca/category/item/154-mobility-and-government-how-to-meet-the-challenge.html

Langford, J., & Roy, J. (2008). *Moving towards cross-boundary citizen-centred service delivery: Challenges and lessons from Canada and around the world.* Washington, DC: IBM Center for the Business of Government.

Langford, J., & Roy, J. (2009). Service transformation, public-private partnerships & shared accountability? Emerging ideas and new practices in B.C., Canada. *International Journal of Public Policy, 4*(3), 232–250.

LeBlanc, J. (2012). Connecting beyond boundaries. *Canadian Government Executive, 17*(8). Retrieved from: http://www.canadiangovernmentexecutive.ca/category/item/141.html

Lee, G., & Kwak, Y. (2011). *An open government implementation model: Moving to increased public engagement.* Washington, DC: IBM Center for The Business of Government.

Lehrer, J. (2012). *Imagine: How creativity works.* New York: Houghton Mifflin Harcourt Publishing Company.

Lips, M. (2012). E-government is dead: Long live public adminstration 2.0. *Information Polity, 17*(2012), 239–250.

Losse, K. (2012). *The boy kings: A journey into the heart of the social network.* New York: Simon & Schuster.

Lowe, G. (2006). High trust workplaces support service excellence. *Canadian Government Executive.* Retrieved from: http://www.grahamlowe.ca/documents/155/CGE%20high%20trust%20workplaces%20Oct-06.pdf.

Lundy, K. (2010). *CeBIT 2010: Gov 2.0 building a strong foundation for open democracy.* Retrieved from http://www.katelundy.com.au/2010/03/02/cebit-2010-gov-2-0-building-a-strong-foundation-for-open-democracy/

MacGillis, Al. (2012). No one is 'playing politics' on Solyndra or birth control. This is politics. Washington Post, February 24, 2012.

Macintosh, A. (2003). Using Information and Communications Technologies to Enhance Citizen Engagement in the Policy Process. *Promise and Problems of E-Democracy: Challenges of Online Engagement.* Paris: OECD.

Macmillan, P., Medd, A., & Hughes, P. (2008). *Change your world or the world will change you: The future of collaborative government and Web 2.0.* Deloitte. Retrieved from: http://www.deloitte.com/assets/Dcom-Canada/Local%20Assets/Documents/ca_govt_web20_mar08_EN.pdf.

Maier-Rabler, U., & Huber, S. (2011). "Open": The changing relation between citizens, public administration, and political authority. *JeDEM: Journal of Democracy, 3*(2), 182–191.

Maio, A. D. (2009). *Cloud computing may become the worst enemy of centralization.* Retrieved from Gartner Blog: http://blogs.gartner.com/andrea_dimaio/2009/08/05/cloud-computing-may-become-the-worst-enemy-of-centralization/

Martin, L. (2010). *Harperland: The politics of control.* Toronto, ON: Penguin Group Canada.

Mayeda, A., & Miller, H. (2012). *Secret memo warns of Canadian cyber threat after Nortel attack.* Retrieved from Financial Post: http://business.financialpost.com/2012/06/06/secret-memo-warns-of-canadian-cyber-threat-after-nortel-attack/

McNutt, K. (2009). *Citizen engagement through online consultation a comment on public involvement and e-consultation: A new era of democratic governance in Canada.* Montreal, QC: IRPP.

McNutt, K. A., & Carey, M. (2008). *Canadian digital government.* Regina: Saskatchewan Institute of Public Policy.

McNutt, K., & Pal, L. (2011). "Modernizing Government": Mapping Global Public Policy Networks. *Governance, 24*(3), 439–467.

Meijer, A. J. (2011). Networked Coproduction of public services in virtual communities: From a government-centric to a community approach to public service support. *Public Administration Review, 7*, 598–607.

Mergel, I. (2012a). *Working the network: A manager's guide for using twitter in government.* Washington, DC: IBM Center for The Business of Government.

Mergel, I. (2012b). *A manager's guide to designing a social media strategy.* Washington, DC: IBM Center for The Business of Government.

Mindus, P., Greppi, A., & Cuono, M. (2011). *Legitimacy 2.0—E-democracy and public opinion in the digital age* (p. 182). Frankfurt am Main: Goethe University Press.

Mossberger, K., & Wu, Y. (2012). *Civic engagement and local e-government: Social networking comes of age.* Chicago, IL: UIC Institute for Policy and Civic Engagement.

Mota, J. C., & Santinha, G. (2012). Social media and civic engagement: Discussing the case of Aveiro Portugal. *European Journal of ePractice, 16.*

Nabatchi, T. (2010). Addressing the citizenship and democratic deficits: The potential of deliberative democracy for public administration. *The American Review of Public Administration, 40*(4), 376–399.

OECD. (2001). *The hidden threat to E-government: Avoiding large government IT failures.* Paris: OECD.

Oliveira, M. (2012). *Canada's 'most socially networked' title slipping away.* Retrieved from the Globe and Mail: http://www.theglobeandmail.com/technology/digital-culture/social-web/canadas-most-socially-networked-title-slipping-away/article550205/

Orr, A. (2010). *Blogging, deliberation and the public sphere.* University of New South Wales, School of Social Science and International Studies. Retrieved from: http://www.polsis.uq.edu.au/docs/Challenging-Politics-Papers/Allison-Orr-Blogging-Deliberation-and-the-Public-Sphere.pdf

Osimo, D. (2008). *Web 2.0 in government: Why and how?* Luxembourg: European Commission Joint Research Centre.

Owens, J. (2012). *Welcome to the Political Sphere Facebook Generation! iPolitics.* Retrieved from: http://www.ipolitics.ca/2012/02/23/jordan-owens-welcome-to-the-politicalsphere-facebook-generation/

Owens, R. C. (2010). Noises heard: Canada's recent online copyright consultation process—Teachings and cautions. IPOSGOODE. Retrieved from: http://www.iposgoode.ca/wp-content/uploads/2010/04/RichardOwens_Online_Copyright_Consultation_19April2010.pdf

Paquet, G. (1997). States, communities and markets: The distributed governance scenario. In T. J. Courchene (Ed.), *The nation-state in a global information era: Policy challenges the bell Canada papers in economics and public policy* (pp. 25–46). Kingston, ON: John Deutsch Institute for the Study of Economic Policy.

Paquet, G. (2004). There is more to governance than public candelabras: E-governance and Canada's public service. In L. Oliver & L. Sanders (Eds.), *E-government reconsidered: Renewal of governance for the knowledge age.* Regina: Canadian Plains Research Center.

Paquet, G., & Roy, J. (1995). Prosperity through networks: The bottom-up strategy that might have been. In S. Philips (Ed.), *How Ottawa spends 1995–96 midlife crises* (pp. 137–158). Ottawa, ON: Carleton University Press.

Pogue, D. (2012). *Where is David Pogue's iPhone?* Retrieved from The New York Times: http://pogue.blogs.nytimes.com/2012/08/02/where-is-david-pogues-phone/

Pole, A. (2011). Blogging the political: Politics and participation in a networked. *Government Information Quarterly, 28,* 290–293.

Ponemon (2011). *Global survey on social media risks: Survey of IT & IT security practitioners in Canada.* The Ponemon Institute. Retrieved from: http://www.websense.com/content/ponemon-institute-research-report-2011.aspx

Press, J. (2013). *Legal threats over lost student loan SIN numbers may finally push government to better secure data.* Retrieved from National Post: http://news.nationalpost.com/2013/01/18/legal-threats-over-lost-student-loan-sin-numbers-may-finally-push-government-to-better-secure-data/

Public Accounts Committee. (2012). *Public accounts committee—Tenth report implementing the transparency agenda.* UK: British House of Commons.

Public Administration Committee. (2011). *Twelfth report—Government and IT: "A Recipe For Rip-Offs": Time for a new approach.* London: Parliament of Great Britain.

Public Policy Forum. (2012). *Building youth engagement through civic collaboration.* Ottawa, ON: Public Policy Forum.

Quigley, K., & Roy, J. (2011). Cyber-security and risk management in an interoperable world: An examination of governmental action in North America. *Social Sciences Computer Review, 30*(1), 83–94.

Raduege. (2011). Top Three 2012 Cybersecurity "Game-Changers." Retrieved online from: http://www.washingtonexec.com/2011/12/lt-general-harry-raduege-top-three-2012-cybersecurity-game-changers/

Reddick, C. G. (2011). Customer Relationship Management (CRM) technology and organizational change: Evidence for the bureaucratic and e-government paradigms. *Government Information Quarterly, 28*, 346–353.

Reddick, C. G., & Aikins, S. K. (Eds.). (2012). *Web 2.0 technologies and democratic governance: Political, policy and management implications.* New York: Springer.

Reddick, C. G., & Roy, J. (2013). Business perceptions and satisfaction with E-government: Findings from a Canadian Survey. *Government Information Quarterly, 30*(1), 1–9.

Reid, J. (2004). Holding Governments Accountable by Strengthening Access to Information Laws and Information Management Practices. In Oliver, L. and Sanders, L., Eds. (2004) *E-Government Reconsidered: Renewal of Governance for the Knowledge Age.* Regina: Canadian Plains Research Center.

Reinwald, A., & Kraemmergaard, P. (2011, March 17–18). Managing stakeholders in transformational government—A case study in a Danish local government. *tGov Workshop '11 (tGOV11).* West London: Brunel University.

Ritchel, M. (2010) Growing Up Digital, Wired for Distraction. New York Times. Accessed online: http://www.nytimes.com/2010/11/21/technology/21brain.html?_r=0&adxnnl=1&ref=yourbrai noncomputers&adxnnlx=1367238698-ZxbokT5qr2J1eSPbBiaAtA

Roberts, A. (2006). *Blacked out—Government secrecy in the information age.* New York: Cambridge University Press.

Roberts, N. C. (2011). Beyond smokestacks and silos: Open-source, Web-Enabled Coordination in Organizations and Networks. *Public Administration Review, 71*, 677–693.

Rogers, B. (2005). From membership to management? The future of political parties as democratic organizations. *Parliamentary Affairs, 58*(3), 600–610.

Roman, F., Koster, A., Le Merle, M., & Petersen, M. (2010). The rise of generation C: Implications for the World of 2020. New York: booz@co.

Roy, J. (2006). *E-government in Canada: Transformation for the digital age* (Governance Series). Ottawa, ON: University of Ottawa Press.

Roy, J. (2008). Beyond Westminster governance: Bringing politics and public service into the network era. *Canadian Public Administration, 5*(4), 541–568.

Roy, J. (2010). *The rise of networked governance everywhere but in Westminster democracy. Policy options, September, 2010.* Montreal, QC: Institute for Research on Public Policy.

Roy, J. (2011). *Bridging the great divide: Pliticians and the public.* Montreal, QC: IRPP.

Roy, J. (2012a). Social media's democratic paradox: Lessons from Canada. *European Journal of ePractice, 16*, 5–15.

Roy, J. (2012b). E-government & the evolution of service Canada—Transformation or stagnation? In C. G. Reddick (Ed.), *Public sector transformation through E-government: Experiences from Europe and North America.* London: Routledge.

Roy, J. (2012c). Secrecy versus openness: Democratic adaptation in a Web 2.0 era. In C. G. Reddick & S. K. Aikins (Eds.), *Web 2.0 technologies and democratic governance: Political, policy and management implications.* New York: Springer.

Roy, J. (2013). E-government & the evolution of service Canada—Transformation or stagnation? In C. G. Reddick (Ed.), *Public sector transformation through E-government: Experiences from Europe and North America.* London: Routledge.

Rubin, J. (2010) Why Your World is About to Get a Whole Lot Smaller. Toronto: Random House.

Salusinszky, I. (2012). *Faith in political leaders collapses according to Newspoll survey.* Retrieved from The Australian: National Affairs: http://www.theaustralian.com.au/national-affairs/faith-in-political-leaders-collapses-according-to-newspoll-survey/story-fn59niix-1226518493021

Samara. (2010). *It's my party: Parliamentary dysfunction reconsidered. The third in a series of reports exploring political leadership in Canada*. Toronto, ON: Samara Research Institute.

Savoie, D. J. (1999) *Governing from the Centre: The Concentration of Power in Canadian Politics*. Toronto: University of Toronto Press.

Schick, S. (2011). *Lac carling: Belgian IT ministry shows off electronic IDs*. Retrieved from IT World Canada: http://www.itworldcanada.com/news/lac-carling-belgian-it-ministry-shows-off-electronic-ids/143145

Schon, D. (1971). *Beyond the stable state*. New York: Random House.

Serrat, P. (2010). *Social media and the public sector*. Manila: Asian Development Bank.

Shane, P. M. (Ed.). (2004). *Democracy online: The prospects for political renewal through the internet*. London: Routledge.

Shirky, C. (2008). *Here comes everybody: The power of organizing without organizations*. New York: Penguin Group.

Shirky, C. (2011). The political power of social media. *Foreign Affairs*. Council of Foreign Relations.

Sloam, J. (2007). Rebooting democracy: Youth participation in politics in the UK. *Parliamentary Affairs, 60*, 548–567.

Smith, A. (2011). *The internet and campaign 2010*. Washington, DC: Pew Research Institute.

Sommer, L., & Cullen, R. (2009). Participation 2.0: A case study of e-participation within the New Zealand Government. *42nd Hawaii international conference on system sciences*, Hawaii: Systems Sciences 2009, pp. 1–10.

Stoker, G. (2005). Public value management—A new narrative for networked governance? *American Review of Public Administration, 36*(1), 41–57.

Takhteyev, Y., Gruzd, A., & Wellman, B. (2012). Geography of twitter networks. *Social Networks, Special issue on Space and Networks, 34*(1), 73–81.

Tapscott, D., & Williams, A. (2006). *WIKINOMICS—How mass collaboration changes everything*. New York: Penguin Group.

Thomas, P. (2008). Political Administrative Interface in Canada's Public Sector. *Optimum Online, 38*(2), 21–26.

Timberg, C. (2012) *Refugee from Facebook questions the social media life*. Washington Post. Retrieved from: http://articles.washingtonpost.com/2012-08-03/business/35491933_1_facebook-board-member-katherine-losse-facebook-homepage.

Timoshenko, L. & Demers, J. (2012) Social Media Use Among Ontario Municipalities is Growing Fast. Redbrick Communications (Toronto). Accessed online at: http://www.redbrick.ca/assets/file/resource/Social-Media-Growth.pdf

Treadwell, J. (2007). *Shared Governance and Collaboration. Prepared for EDUCAUSE Australasia 2007—Advancing knowledge pushing boundaries*. Melbourne, Australia. 21–26

Ubaldi, B. C. (2011). The impact of the economic and financial crisis on E-Government in OECD member countries. *European Journal of ePractise, 11*, 1–14.

Ubaldi, B. C., & Roy, J. (2010). E-government and federalism in Italy and Canada—A comparative assessment. In C. Reddick (Ed.), *Comparative E-government* (pp. 183–200). New York: Springer.

United Nations Economic and Social Council. (2007). *Participatory governance and citizens' engagement in policy development*. New York: Service Delivery and Budgeting.

United States Office of Personnel Management. (2012). *Status of telework in the federal government*. Washington, DC: United States Office of Personnel Management. Retrieved from: http://www.telework.gov/Reports_and_Studies/Annual_Reports/2012teleworkreport.pdf

Viitanen, J. (2010). *Does transparency erode trust?* The Guardian.

Wanna, J., & O'Flynn, J. (2008). *Collaborative governance: Collaborative governance*. Australia: The Australian National University Press.

Ware, J., & Grantham, C. (2010). *Managing a remote workforce: Proven practices from successful leaders*. The Work Design Collaboration, LLC. Retrieved from: http://www.thefutureofwork.net/assets/Managing_Remote_Workforce_Proven_Practices.pdf

Weerakkody, V. & Reddick, C.G. (2011). Public sector transformation through E-Government: Experiences from Europe and North America. Routledge: New York.

Williams, A. D. (2012). Government 2.0: Wikinomics and the Challenge to Government. *Canadian Government Executive, 14*(1). Retrieved from: http://www.canadiangovernmentexecutive.ca/innovation/item/730-government-20-wikinomics-and-the-challenge-to-government.html

World Economic Forum. (2011). *The future of government: Lessons learned from around the World.* World Economic Forum: Global Agenda Council on the Future of Government.

Wyld, D. (2007). *The blogging revolution: Government in the age of Web 2.0.* Washington, DC: IBM Endowment for The Business of Government.

Wyld, D. C. (2010a). *Moving to the cloud: An introduction to cloud computing in government.* Washington, DC: IBM Center for The Business of Government.

Wyld, D. C. (2010b). THE cloudy future of government IT: Cloud computing and the public sector around the world. *International Journal of Web & Semantic Technology, 1*(1).

Young, N. (2012). *The virtual self.* Toronto, ON: McClelland & Stewart.

Index

CPSIA information can be obtained at www.ICGtesting.com
Printed in the USA
LVOW11*1938281113

363111LV00013B/79/P

9 781461 472209

0 1341 1464671 1

DATE DUE	RETURNED